DEAN LAZAR'S GOLDEN GUIDE

Pragmatic Career Advice for Smart Young People

DEAN LAZAR'S GOLDEN GUIDE

Pragmatic Career Advice for Smart Young People

Lydia Lazar

NIRA 1920 LLC

Chicago, Illinois

Interior text design by Mallori Stone

Library of Congress Cataloging-in-Publication Data

Lazar, Lydia, 1959–

Dean Lazar's Golden Guide: Pragmatic Career Advice for Smart Young People / Lydia Lazar. – NIRA 1920 LLC

ISBN-13: 978-0-9996220-0-1

1. Career Development   2. Success in Business   I. Title

Dedicated to my mother
Judith Axelrood Herman
1931–2009
and
In honor of my daughters
Rachel and Naomi

Contents

Acknowledgments   **xiii**

Preface   **xiv**

Welcome   **xvi**

Chapter One: Stepping Into Your Career

Let's Get Started!   1

Step One: Identifying and Developing Your Interests and Skills   1

   Use the Resources Available to You   2

   What Interests You Professionally?   2

   Key Skill Sets   6

Step Two: Matching Your Interests to the Available Opportunities   7

   Explore Your Options   7

   Work with Career Services   8

   Be Intentional   9

Step Three: Stepping Into Your Career   10

   Enhance Your Appearance   11

   Improve Your Self-Presentation   12

      Unplug and Practice Small Talk with Strangers   13

      Practice Introducing Yourself   13

      Watch Your Tone   14

   How to Develop Your Narrative(s) and Your Elevator Speech   14

   Developing a Great Elevator Speech   18

   Evolving Your Narratives   19

Step Four: Finding Your Niche in the Opportunity Ecosystem   20

   Networking Like a Pro   21

      Game Plan to Reach Out Through Your Inner Circle   23

      Game Plan to Reach Out to Strangers   25

      Writing Short Friendly Outreach Emails   26

Business Cards   27

Introducing Yourself at Networking Parties and Events   28

Making Yourself Memorable   29

A Personal Board of Directors: The Secret of Successful People   30

Creating Your Professional Reputation   31

Chapter One Take-Aways   33

Chapter Two: Thriving in a Social Media World

Life in the Digital Age   35

One: Honestly Inventory Your Online Presence   36

Two: Revisit Your Privacy Settings For All Sites   38

Three: Enhance Your Personal Brand   39

Key Defensive Steps to Take   40

Clean Up Your Digital Footprint   40

Remove Third Party Content   41

De-Index Social Accounts   42

Delete Some Accounts   42

Key Pro-active Steps to Take   43

Finish/Complete all Profiles   43

Market Yourself Online   44

Chapter Two Take-Aways   45

Chapter Three: Presenting Your Best Self

Getting in the Game   47

Finding Opportunities   48

Selling Yourself to Others   49

Writing a Great Cover Letter or Outreach Email   50

Cover Letter Structure   51

Recipient Address and Greeting   52

Content of the Letter   52

Crafting a Winning Resume   54

Resume Do's   55

Resume Don'ts   56

Comparing a Curriculum Vitae (C.V.) to a Resume   56

Sample Opportunity: Entry Level Marketing Assistant   57

Sample Cover Letters and Resumes   59

Job Interviewing Tips and Strategies   63

3 Key Tips for Interview Success   66

Writing a Timely and Smart Thank You Note   66

    Purpose and Format of a Smart Follow up Email   67

    Sample Thank You Notes   68

What About Your References?   69

Getting Better All the Time: More Training, New Credentials   70

What about Nontraditional Credentials?   73

    MOOCs   74

    Online and Low Residency Degree Programs   75

What Sort of Training Should Everyone Consider Obtaining?   76

Staying Relevant and Competitive   77

Chapter Three Take-Aways   78

Chapter Four: Finding Your Place in The Real World of Work

Identifying Opportunities   81

    On Campus Recruiting: Is It Worth the Time?   82

    Staying Relevant: In Person Networking   82

    What Sort of Organizational Role Should You Seek?   83

    When to Work for Big Institutions, and Why   85

    Finding Jobs with Established Companies and Organizations   87

Overcoming Obstacles   89

    Obstacles to Getting Hired by Organizations   89

    Strategies for Overcoming HR Obstacles   91

      Be Known   91

      Get an Internal Referral   92

      Connect at All Levels   93

    How to Make a Phone Call   94

Learning to Succeed   95

    Benefits of Working with Established Companies and Organizations   96

    Working with and for Start Ups   97

    Nonprofit Organizations   99

    Social Entrepreneurs   100

    You are Always Working for Yourself   100

Succeeding in Multicultural and Diverse Work Places   102

Expressing Yourself at Work   103

Chapter Four Take-Aways   105

Chapter Five: Enhancing Your Personal Resilience

Hiking without a Map   107

The Real Power of Positive Thinking: Framing and Re-Framing your Experiences   109

Staying Competitive, Agile, and Relevant   110

Building Resilience: 9 Key Habits of Mind and Body   112

    1. Compete at Peak Physical and Mental Health   112

    2. Develop and Use Self Care Strategies   113

    3. Integrate Technology Best Practices   117

       Schedule and Take Technology Breaks   118

       Practice Good Technology Hygiene   119

    4. Use Discretion To Compete in the Real World   120

    5. Circulate and Be Known to Others in the Office   122

    6. Always Be Learning   123

       Learn Across Multiple Fields   124

       Cultivate Your Critical Thinking Skills   125

       Practice Thinking Outside the Box   126

    7. Cultivate Your Non-Cognitive Skills and Character traits   128

    8. Learn to Accept Feedback and Course Correct   131

       Feedback at Work: Use Extreme Caution   132

    9. Build Resilience Through Relationships   134

Chapter Five Take-Aways   135

Chapter Six: Creating Your Life, Not Just Your Career

Stay Relevant as the World of Work Automates   138

Keep Yourself Employable: Schedule Regular Self Reviews   139

Reach Out For Support   140

    Use Your Inner Circle as a Sounding Board   140

    Continue to Build Your Personal Board of Directors   140

Helping Others Will Help You Succeed   141

Being Authentic   141

Avoiding Careerism   143

Driving Your Career Forward   144

Be Self Aware: Proud + Humble, Confident + Open Minded   145

Consider Your Circumstances of Birth a Reality Check, Not a Limit   145

Career and Life Arcs   147

Having It All   149

Making a Difference   150

Getting Paid to Think + Thinking About Things that Matter to You   152

Resource File: Notes and Additional Reading   **155**

Resource File: Internet Sites   **159**

Resource File: Key Skill Sets   **167**

Resource File: Advice for International Students   **173**

Resource File: Applying for Graduate School   **181**

Resource File: Writing Style Guide   **197**

Resource File: Dean Lazar's Golden Tips   **215**

Index   **223**

Acknowledgments

Early readers gave me extraordinary, invaluable feedback that helped me re-frame the narrative. Thanks to Maude Carroll, Paul Dillon, Joel Epstein, Jullie Han, Alison Hoffman, Naomi Lazar, Rachel Lazar, Nadine Pearce, Toni Riccardi, Tracy Samantha Schmidt, Rebecca Sive, Marge Stockford, Andrew Ting, and Brandea Turner. Any and all mistakes that remain are, of course, mine alone.

Previous versions of some of the material in Chapters One and Three, and in the RF: Internet Sites, appeared in handouts I wrote and/or edited with the career services team, Jandi Kelly and Leslie Andersen, at the University of Chicago's Harris School of Public Policy.

For general layout and design assistance, great thanks to Joe Grossman and his firm Jell Creative, and to the unflappable Mallori Stone.

I have benefited over my entire career from wide ranging conversations with my former bosses, colleagues and students, my close friends, and my mentors, including Insa Blanke, Michele Cohen, Barry Commoner, Ernie and Jeri Drucker, Joel Epstein, Ed Falkman, Martha Frish, Robert Graff, Alison Hoffman, Mindy Kallus, Candice Kline, Harold Krent, Bart Lazar, Robert Jason Liff, Nancy Martin, Nadine Pearce, Stephani Perlmutter, Henry Perritt, Stephen Quatrano, Abbey Romanek, Susan Salzberg, Alan Schoor, Frank Schroeder, Paula Sjogerman, Dominika Smereczynski, Marge Stockford, Marty and Mercedes Straus, David Thompson, Gavino Villapiano, Isabel Wade, and Frances Whitehead.

My mother's straightforward approach to the world of work had a powerful influence on me, and her perspective is reflected in much of the advice here. Finally, writing this book would not have been possible without the loving encouragement and support of my daughters Rachel and Naomi, and of my husband, David Klein.

Preface

Are you a person who wants to be intellectually challenged at work, but you are not 100% sure of what direction you want your career to take?

Do you want to help solve the difficult challenges our world faces, but do not know what you want to do — much less how to make a living doing it??

Many young people seeking employment opportunities and career advancement today feel overwhelmed and underprepared for the challenges they face as they leave college and enter the workforce. There is a lot of apparently conflicting advice, and the constant media barrage about the decline and transformation of the U.S. economy can depress even the most optimistic job seeker.

Today's college students can brilliantly navigate the world through smartphone technology—yet many digital natives are frustrated and intimidated when it comes to creating in-person real world relationships. The good news is that there are skills and behaviors that you can learn to help you leverage your digital social world to create the professional relationships you need to have as you face an increasingly competitive work world.

This Golden Guide is designed for all young people who want to find opportunities to be *paid to think* and to continue to develop their skills, while also making a contribution to the work of a larger enterprise. Thanks to the digital technologies that are changing everything about how employers recruit and screen for new employees, *even the most well educated and self-disciplined young people are scrambling to find substantive full time work opportunities.* When every opening receives thousands and even tens of thousands of applicants, the odds of getting past the gate-keepers and into an interview are truly daunting.

As you move from job to job and into progressively more challenging and responsible roles in different organizations, you will face a rapidly chang-ing world of work. Successful careers in the 21st century will follow different trajectories than in the past, but successful people will always be those who go after what they want with grace and humility. I want to help you *now and for years to come,* so this Guide is focused on how you can develop a set of *habits of mind and behavior*—your own personal, *best practices*—that will serve you throughout your career.

The expression **"Luck is what happens when preparation meets opportunity"** is attributed to the Roman philosopher Seneca. By incor-porating these habits of mind and behavior into your life at an early age, you will not only prepare yourself to be lucky in your career: you will set yourself on course for a fulfilling, satisfying life.

Welcome

Congratulations on deciding to take control of your time, your energy and your attention as you focus on achieving your career objectives. No matter where you are in terms of your education or your career, this Golden Guide can help you. The suggestions and advice in these pages will guide you along the path to realizing your dreams…and with luck, over time, you will find an intellectually challenging job and develop an emotionally and financially rewarding career.

We live in a world where getting paid to think is not a guaranteed outcome for even the most highly educated people. There will be competition at every step of your academic and professional life. To succeed and prosper, you must be smart, prepared and lucky. You must also be ambitious and persistent, and you must continually seek out new skills and new opportunities to be challenged.

You may have been told that to find a job, you must study the STEM subjects (Science, Technology, Engineering or Math.) While it is certainly true that there are many opportunities in STEM fields, those are not the only careers worth pursuing. This Guide is for all students, regardless of major. The strategies described here to help you advance in your career will apply to all industries and all employers.

- In Chapter One, you will find foundational suggestions for specific actions to take as you begin to define yourself as a young professional.
- In Chapter Two we take an in depth look at strategies for handling the important, invasive and risky world of social media.
- In Chapter Three, I offer some detailed advice for resume, cover and thank you letter writing, for acing job interviews, and for thinking about additional credentials throughout your career.

- Chapter Four explores different kinds of organizations, the roles you might find in them, and smart strategies to defeat obstacles and get hired.
- Chapters Five and Six provide guidance for navigating the working world — how to deal with the ups and downs of daily life, and how to think creatively about the life and career you are building for yourself.

At the end of the book there are some specialized resource pages, including a section on applying to U.S. graduate schools and another with specific, targeted advice for international students studying in the U.S.

Spread throughout the book, you will find **Dean Lazar's Golden Tips** — short, memorable messages that can help you stay focused and productive.

1 | Stepping Into Your Career

Let's Get Started!

You *can* find opportunities to do challenging work, get paid a reasonable wage, and keep developing your skill set. How? By taking a few steps every day to prepare yourself to succeed. This means being *intentional* about how you spend your time, and *focused* as you cultivate expertise in different subjects.

Step One: Identifying Your Interests and Skills

Starting now, you must honestly examine your interests, your strengths, your challenges and your dreams. *Only you can know which subjects and activities really engage your mind and your heart.* To succeed, you must face your fears, embrace your passions and take a few steps forward every day, every month, and every semester. If you nurture your intellectual and professional capabilities in this way you will definitely find a job and a career that will both suit you and thrill you!

If you are already a senior in college, or a recent graduate, or even studying in a graduate degree program, the same advice applies to you as to younger undergraduates. You will grow professionally only if you continue to increase your self-awareness and stay honest with yourself about your evolving interests and passions. Many jobs do not turn out as we expect; one important early career lesson is that we learn a lot about ourselves as we move through positions and organizations, and what interested us as students may be less compelling as we grow into our twenties.

Golden Tip #2
**Use the Resources
Available to You.**
If you are already out of school,
go to the library or a local
bookstore. Look around for
mentors and advisors in your
workplace and community.
There is wisdom and
experience all around you.

Use the Resources Available to You

Explore all the career support services your school offers. Don't hesitate to go back multiple times to the office, and consider meeting with more than one counselor or staffer, as different people may suggest diverse resources to you.

Cultivate relationships on campus: you are surrounded by scholarly professionals who are committed to helping young people discover their full potential! Be gracious and appreciative of their time.

Meet your professors during office hours and, in a polite and professional way, ask them about their careers, their research, current controversies in their field, and how they see their field changing.

Tell professors and others you meet on campus about your interests and ask them what career advice they might have for you, given your interests.

What Interests You Professionally?

You have probably identified an academic major, but have you taken the time to consider what you truly enjoy thinking about and what professions will enable you to continue your intellectual explorations? It can be a challenge to identify your professional interests, and you should spend a fair amount of time thinking about this, since you want to make sure that you are preparing yourself for a career that you will enjoy.

One place to start is in the Bureau of Labor Statistics data on different industries and professions. In this free U.S. government data set, you can learn about many different industries. For each industry, you can find information about working conditions, specific occupations within the industry, training and advancement, earnings and benefits, and the current employment outlook. See the **Resource File: Internet Sites**.

I strongly recommend that you go to talk with a career counselor. Although many students dislike going to their career services offices, if you approach the team there with an open mind, I am sure you can find something useful from the encounter. Career exploration conversations should be fun—after all, the point is to dream and fantasize about your future life, with the shared goal of identifying resources to help you realize your aspirations.

In addition to speaking one-on-one with a counselor, you should make sure you are aware of the other services the career office provides. For example, your career services office probably offers talks, usually entitled something like "Exploring Careers in [profession]" and often featuring a guest speaker from a particular employer who is recruiting at your school. Take the opportunity to learn firsthand about different fields by attending these talks and asking the speakers about their careers.

One very important thing to keep in mind is that, in general, there is not really a specific major that matches a specific professional career. While it is true that there are some professions (like nursing or architecture) that require the very specific skills taught in particular undergraduate programs, *most majors can lead to a variety of professions and career opportunities.*

This is because the world's jobs, in fact, are not organized by academic discipline.

With good writing, analytical thinking and research skills, all graduates can find work. There is a wide variety of industries, a range of employers within those industries, and many different job functions even within the most technically oriented companies. The primary challenge for young professionals at the start their careers is to identify subject(s) that interest them enough to pursue and succeed at a position as an entry level employee.

As discussed in more detail later in the Guide, the careers of the 21st century will be different from those of the past century in many ways. Successful people will be those who:

- Are **strong communicators** who can combine information from different formats and interpret it to make persuasive narratives and arguments,
- Can **adapt quickly** to changing circumstances,
- Can **anticipate challenges** and opportunities before they arise, and
- Have **strong interpersonal skills** and can appropriately interpret social and emotional cues.

STEM majors (Science, Technology, Engineering or Math) often seem to have clearer paths to employment, with technically oriented companies seeking their particular technical skills for entry-level positions. However even STEM majors don't work solely with those technical "hard" skills, and to succeed in the work world they will need to be able to communicate just as well as their non-STEM colleagues.

Humanities majors (such as English, History, Comparative Literature or Philosophy students) may seem to have less obvious career paths, but this is really a strength—not a weakness—of these students. As later chapters explain in more detail, the *careers of today's young professionals are going to be defined by the capacity to learn new skills and communicate effectively with colleagues and clients, and Humanities majors should excel in these domains.*

Talk with your counselor about as many industries and roles as you can, and do not hesitate to **actively plan out several possible career paths.** You are a smart, creative person and there are there are many different fields and job functions to consider as you begin your career exploration.

Whatever your major, consider pursuing positions as varied as marketing, product development, journalism, education, project management, counseling, consulting, sales, fundraising, recruitment, commercial business, arts administration, nonprofit program management, operations analysis or even market research for a multinational corporation. There really is no limit to what you can do with your life, if you face the future with a sense of personal agency and an optimistic spirit.

Try to visit the career services resource library when you have at least 45–60 minutes to read around in the books and other resources. You will find a variety of materials that you can review to learn about different professions, industries, companies and organizations. It's likely that you will learn about fields you never knew about, and that you will want to schedule a return visit — or two. **Give yourself enough time to really explore the many diverse professions and fields that hire college graduates.**

Identifying your interests is the first step toward developing your professional capacity. The next step is to understand which skills those jobs require, and frankly assess how prepared you are for the entry level positions you will be seeking. Your strategy as you do this personal assessment is to:

- think as broadly as you can about your existing abilities and experiences,
- clarify those skills that you have already developed, and
- identify the skills you need to cultivate to ensure that you will be a strong candidate for the positions you seek.

Remember: no one was born with any of these skills! Everyone has to develop them, and you may as well start while you are in school to grow your skill set(s) so you will be competitive for the jobs you want.

**Golden Tip #3
You Drive the CAR
in Your Career.**

Cultures and families are different, and some people feel obligated to pursue the profession chosen for them by their families. Whether or not you are paying your own college tuition, you are the person who will be living your life, and you must drive the career car.

Your personal objective, as you look for post-graduate employment, is to be hired into positions where you can *learn on the job* and *develop new skills* as you mature. Keep in mind that successful professionals identify and work to develop the skills corresponding to the positions they hope to obtain *next*—that is, after they master the job they have now. If you are intentional and thoughtful, you can strengthen your mastery of those skills that really interest and motivate you so that you will be qualified and able to move up as you move on to another job, company or even industry.

Throughout this Guide I will offer suggestions for continuing to strengthen your skill sets so you can stay competitive as the world of work changes around you.

Key Skill Sets

There are four key areas where employers expect applicants to demonstrate their skills—and these skill sets are applied in a wide range of industries and at all levels of employment from entry level to senior management. The four key skill sets are:

- analytical and problem solving skills
- written and verbal communication skills
- project management skills
- interpersonal skills

These are not the only skills in the work world, but they are foundational for work that requires *thinking*—and that's the work that you want to do. At the end of the day, people hire for "competence plus fit" so you need to be sure that you are continuing to *master the specific skills that employers in your field are looking for*—even as you build out all your other social and professional skills.

In **Chapter Three** we will review how to be a competitive applicant for the positions that interest you. For example, you will see that you need to make sure that your resume and social media profiles—such as on Linked In or Twitter—highlight *your specific skills within these skill sets*.

In the **Resource File: Key Skill Sets** at the back of this Guide you will find detailed phrases that you should modify to describe your specific skills and experiences. Take the time to review the skill sets and think creatively about your experiences and capabilities.

Once you can describe your own interests and skills *using the words and phrases that match the language that employers use to describe their open positions*, you will search much more effectively for jobs and be a more competitive applicant.

Step Two: Matching Your Interests to the Available Opportunities

As you will learn later in this Guide, the discovery of new opportunities as you move ahead in your career is most strongly correlated with the amount of networking you do, and spending too much time searching for job opportunities on the Internet can be counterproductive and demoralizing. However—and especially when you are exploring career options—*the Internet is an incredible research resource* that you should use to learn about how your interests and skills match up with what is out there in the world of work.

Explore Your Options

Use the Internet to broaden your knowledge of professions and industries. Be intentional about this research and keep track of the companies and job titles that you discover. Be as open minded as you can be: imagine your dream career and think big! After all, if you don't know anything about a profession, you can't know if you might enjoy it. Give yourself permission to fantasize and to dream—but be sure to stay grounded in the reality of real jobs.

Look at all the different job titles on **Indeed.com** or another job board or website and review the job responsibilities for the jobs that interest you. Note the kinds of skills that are needed to accomplish the tasks and responsibilities, and the language the employers are using to describe those skills. You can start with some of the job board sites in **Resource File: Internet Sites**.

It is important to keep track of websites and other information you come across in your research. Start a **Career Exploration notebook** or **create a Folder** on your computer where you can save information in Excel spreadsheets or other documents.

Work with Career Services

Also be sure to work with your career counselor to:
- clarify a short list of industries/job titles to explore,
- identify important books and other resources that can help you,
- learn how to access your school's job postings and
- schedule mock interviews and resume reviews.

Most students are surprised by the wide range of industries, employers and jobs that exist—and many are disappointed to discover that they have spent time studying subjects that do not prepare them for the careers they decide they want to pursue. *Remember: picking a major does not mean you cannot study other things, and does not mean you will have only one professional path to follow.*

The advice in this Guide is designed to help you cross the bridge between the end of college or graduate school and the world of work. So if you have decided that you did not learn or are not studying the right thing, don't panic! By thinking about these things now, and working with this Guide, you can develop the skills, contacts and knowledge base to grow into a career that you will love. ***Whatever you have been doing (or not doing) up until now doesn't matter: the important thing is how you think and act going forward.***

And remember that everyone will have multiple jobs—and even multiple careers—over their lifetimes: current thinking suggests that young professionals today are likely to have as many as 15 different jobs by the time they retire. As long as you continually seek out intellectual challenges and pro-actively develop new skills, you will doing all the right things to ensure that you will be lucky and prepared when a new and exciting opportunity presents itself to you.

Be Intentional

Be intentional with your time and your energy. Without realizing it, many people drift along and wait for things to happen to them. They wonder why their friends seem to be doing exciting things or getting great chances in life. In fact, it's far too easy to be complacent when you have gotten into college, or started your first job. The distractions and pleasures of life can fill your days and leave you with no energy or time to search out new challenges.

The truth is, the world doesn't care if you succeed or not. Only those who have your best interests at heart—hopefully your family or a special mentor—care about your happiness and professional achievements. No matter what your circumstances, to be a mature and successful person, you must accept the responsibility to take care of yourself—no matter what happens around you.

So be intentional about your time, your energy and your money. For example, you must manage your financial assets so that you are free to explore new ideas and potential opportunities. This means you must save as much money as you can. If you add up all the money spent in a week on "small things" (like expensive coffee drinks or junk food snacks) and divert just 50% of that money to a savings account, you will start to build a financial cushion that will enable you to make a trip to a new city to explore options, or pay for a course that will help you develop a needed skill.

Golden Tip #4
Be Intentional and Strategic.
The world doesn't care if you succeed or not, so the burden is always on you

- To focus your attention,
- To continually motivate yourself, and
- To take steps that enable you to grow and prosper in your career.

Step Three: Stepping Into Your Career

The best way to build toward the career you want is to start thinking and working as if you already have it. Imagine that every single thing you are doing now is part of your career. Your courses, social activities, creative thinking and even your dreams are all foundational and generative for the person you will become.

As you prepare to leave college and enter the workforce, think about your values and aspirations.

- Aside from earning your way in the world, what do you hope to accomplish with your life?
- What are your expectations for social, economic and personal success?
- Are there particular social or political causes that capture your imagination?
- When you imagine yourself looking back on your life and career many years from now, what do you hope you will see as your achievements—and how do you hope people will describe you and your work?

You may not be able to answer these questions now, but it's a good idea to entertain them—after all, your life's work is far more than just what you do for money. It's the sum of all your actions, interactions, and social contributions—and, as explored more fully in **Chapters Five and Six**, you need to be mindful and intentional so that you do, in fact, integrate your career achievements within a fulfilling life.

It's also important to always keep in mind that, while the world may not care about your career success, *you do need to care about the world*. We all want and need a world that is politically, economically and socially stable. We all need and want a safe and clean environment, and decent communities with good schools. We also need and want societies that are more fair, more just and more caring…and we won't get that world if people focus only on themselves and their careers.

Golden Tip #5
Think Globally, Act Locally.
The world needs you to care about social and economic justice, about natural resources and climate change, and about creating opportunities for everyone in our communities to live decent lives.

This Guide offers you a long term game plan for personal career achievement, however building a successful career doesn't mean you can't also pursue social justice through engaging in, and supporting, social and political activism in your community. Indeed, I urge you to support efforts underway to improve the world around you. You won't regret investing your energy, time and talent this way—and you will enlarge your social circle while contributing to the greater good. Even more importantly, you will be *living your values*—and by staying true to those principles, you will enhance your professional reputation over the long term.

As you gain experience and agency in the world, you will find that the more you align your professional life with your personal values and expectations, the happier and more fulfilled you will be.

The remainder of this Chapter shifts in focus, towards what others may see when they meet you, and the steps you need to take to launch your career. But even as you step up your professional game, you should not neglect inward, reflective thinking.

Enhance Your Appearance

Start with the way you appear and the way you speak about yourself with the people you encounter in your daily life. While we all know we shouldn't judge a book by its cover, you already know that people do make judgments based on the way you look—and your appearance is one of the few things in life that is actually under your control!

So take a deep breath, look in the mirror, and honestly ask yourself: how do I look? Perhaps you could use a good haircut, or take a little more care with your clothes? I am not talking about what to wear to an interview— see **Chapter Three** for that. No, what I am referring to now is your everyday look—how you present yourself to the world around you.

You may be thinking, "Why does my hair style or choice of clothing matter if I am not actually on an interview?" The answer is, it matters because

- you never know who you will meet during your day,
- you cannot know what people are saying about you when you are not around, but you can ensure that one thing they do *not* say is that you dress poorly, or oddly, or worst of all, look unkempt or unprofessional, and
- your online presence will precede any in-person interview with a potential employer. With the prevalence of social media and the likelihood of being filmed or photographed at any event, you want to make sure that when you are tagged in photos, the image enhances your employability!

Other important reasons to pay attention to what you are wearing are that you show the world that you are taking care of yourself, and *you will see yourself* as more professional and more mature. The more seriously you take yourself and your career aspirations, the more seriously others will take you.

Improve Your Self-Presentation

How do you talk about yourself when you are with others? Do you play down your achievements, or refrain from bragging because you think it might offend your friends and acquaintances? Many people fail to put their best foot forward socially and professionally because they are shy, or they are not used to speaking publicly about their activities. In fact, learning to speak in a socially attractive way about what interests you and what you are doing in life is a very important skill that you can and should cultivate.

Of course, social and business cultures around the world are quite varied, so it's very important to appropriately match your self-presentation to the context.

While some people seem to be naturals when it comes to social interaction, no one is born knowing how to socialize or how to advance their career through small talk. You can develop your communications skills and hone your personal presentation skills in many ways. You can enroll in public speaking courses (such as **Dale Carnegie** or **Toastmasters** programs) or participate in teams, clubs, or extracurricular activities where, especially if you seek out leadership positions, you can get practice regularly speaking to groups.

Some students will ask questions in class or use presentations for group assignments to develop confidence when speaking in public. While public speaking and one-to-one social interactions are not exactly the same thing, building confidence in either arena will prepare you for future professional opportunities.

Unplug and Practice Small Talk with Strangers

It can be tempting to spend all your time on your phone when you are in transit or hanging out waiting for a friend. One of the best ways to improve your ability to chat with people is to practice doing so with people you meet randomly. The social stakes are low, and you can end or walk away from the interactions without penalty.

Since many people are plugged into their phones all the time, use your eyes and a smile to determine if someone is open to an exchange with you. You can smile and refer to something in your shared environment— for example, a garbled announcement when you are in transit can open up a conversation if you look up and turn to a neighbor and ask "Did you catch that?"

Practice Introducing Yourself

Everyone needs to learn how to present themselves when introduced to new people. For most business settings in the U.S., it is appropriate to hold out your right hand and introduce yourself by name—unless you are prohibited from doing so by your religious upbringing, or are being introduced to others who may not wish to shake hands.

You should practice holding out your right hand, smiling and shaking hands with a confident, firm handshake, and you should introduce yourself as you shake the other person's hand, by saying something like this:

- Hi, I'm Suzanne Smith, happy to meet you.
- Hi, Suzanne Smith. Good to meet you.
- Hi, nice to meet you, I'm Suzy.

Watch Your Tone

It is important to avoid appearing too self-centered, arrogant or narcissistic; if you tend to be a self-confident, outgoing sort of person, be sure that you take the time to calibrate your approach when meeting new people. Generally, although the world has become more relaxed, *it is always better to err on the more formal end of the spectrum, especially when being introduced to older or more senior people.* Be appropriately deferential, speak briefly and politely, and be sure to listen with an interested look on your face. Listen with your eyes, and smile at the other person!

How to Develop Your Narrative(s) and Your Elevator Speech

You will soon find that there are as many different opportunities to introduce yourself to other people as there are different types of social occasions. You need to develop short introductory narratives that share information about yourself in a gracious and interesting way. As you make your way in the professional and social world, you'll want to have a few short introductions, each slightly different to emphasize different skills, experiences or dreams.

Turn again to the list of transferrable skills in the **Resource File: Key Skill Sets** and start right now to think about all the transferrable skills you have. How will you describe your skills in terms that match the opportunities/industries you want to work in?

Think about your experiences so far and reflect on what you have learned from them about what you like to do. Practice talking about—and positively framing—your internships, jobs and student activities as learning experiences. For more about positive framing, see **Chapter Five: The Real Power of Positive Thinking**.

You can craft short introductions using narrative points thought out ahead of time.

- Golden Tip #18 is **"To fail to prepare is to prepare to fail"**…so sit down periodically and write—and re-write—a *few short phrases and talking points* that you will then have ready in your mind to use when you meet new people.

- Be creative and expansive as you write down potential talking points. A really effective way to get started writing your points is to pretend that you are writing a letter to introduce yourself to someone.

- Try to think of a few different career trajectories for yourself, that are linked in some way to one or more of your current skills or experiences. You are doing this to help yourself think outside the box so that you can imagine multiple possible career paths, with many different jobs along the way.

As you develop your narratives—your short stories of "who I am" and "what I am interested in"—you should *highlight your experiences in terms of the skills you developed and the lessons you learned*.

These narratives—which will certainly change and evolve over the course of your career—are sometimes confused with the similar "elevator speech." The phrase "elevator speech" was coined to describe the hypothetical opportunity to introduce yourself someone important whom you find yourself standing next to in an elevator. See below for an example of how to craft a great elevator speech.

Remember that who you "are" after a few years working is a little different from who you were when you graduated, so your short introductions will certainly need to change over time.

You should always have a few great phrases in your mind that convey a sense of one or more aspects of who you are/what you are interested in.

You should practice saying these phrases and sentences out loud, and you should practice mixing them up so that when you are speaking, they sound natural and upbeat and can convey what you want to say at any particular moment.

Finally, you are NOT reciting your resume bullets in these talking points, but you are using your background to develop *effective personal talking points* that will engage your listener and, hopefully, create an interest in further connection with you.

Here is an example of an exchange where a student has planned ahead what to say when introduced to an alumnus at a social event on campus:

"Hi, Mr. Smith, I'm Andy and I'm also from Chicago."

"Nice to meet you Andy. What are you studying?"

"I'm majoring in Biology and minoring in Communications. I'm very interested in working with science communications somehow—improving the way we talk about important scientific issues like climate change and nuclear power, for example. But I am also thinking about a career in medicine, so I am doing some research for my biology professor—she's an expert on how some cells become cancerous and others don't—and we are looking at possible environmental influences on cancer clusters. I have always been a bit of science geek—I loved science fair in middle and high school."

"Wow, that sounds very interesting Andy. Do you plan to return to Chicago after graduation? Now that the Cubs have broken the curse, it's a great time to be in town."

"I'm not sure, sir. I love my hometown, and my Cubbies, but I also want to explore other cities and even other countries. I am thinking about signing up for the Peace Corps to get some overseas experience. I studied abroad last semester in Costa Rica and really enjoyed getting my Spanish in shape. May I ask what business you are in?"

"Pharmaceutical sales. You know, we hire a lot of biology majors and are always looking for young go-getters. If you do decide to come home to Chicago, here's my card—why don't you look me up in case I might know someone who could help you."

Here is an example of a recent graduate introducing themselves to someone they have just been introduced to at a networking event:

"It's great to meet you John. You know, I really like the way this event brings together folks from different medical fields. I have been working in science communications for a few years, helping XYZ corp. explain the benefits of new drugs and devices to doctors. I started out thinking I'd be a doctor, then I realized that I preferred the business world and with XYZ I've gotten the chance to use my biology and communications degree and Spanish skills— plus travel a lot, which I really enjoy. It's been a wonderful learning experience. Over the past 3 years I have been exploring the capital cities of Latin America and meeting some fantastic doctors working with really diverse populations."

"Wow, that sounds interesting—which city is your favorite?"

"I love Buenos Aires. In fact, I am headed back there next week—there's a tango festival and I have been learning to tango with some friends I met there. In fact, I am thinking about leaving XYZ eventually to start a tango studio in Chicago, my hometown."

"That's fascinating! I love Chicago and I love tango dancing—maybe I can be your first student—or, even better, an investor in your business! Here's my card. Why don't you call me when you are in town and we can grab a drink—and maybe a dance?"

Developing a Great Elevator Speech

An elevator speech is a short but powerful introduction, delivered orally by you, most often to someone who is more senior than you in your company. Your goal is to get them to ask you a question because something you have said has resonated positively with them. The concept is based on the idea that you might find yourself alone in an elevator with someone who is powerful in your world, and you want to make a good impression.

In reality, people don't run into that many important people in elevators, however, if you DO find yourself in an elevator with someone important in your company, and if it is possible to speak to them (no one else is around, the ride is long enough, etc.,) you can introduce yourself by name ("Hi, Mr. Smith, I'm Jeff Jones" or if your company is more informal you can say "Hi John, I'm Jeff Jones") and then say something extremely brief such as:

- *"I am working ["with Cindy and her team on the strategic plan" or "in the marketing department on the new brochure" etc.]*
- *and I am really excited by the chance to ["help imagine future directions for our company" or "develop new markets for the firm" etc]*
- *because of ["my background in market research" or "my passion for finding new customers in the B to B space for our products" or "my interest in corporate communications" etc.].*

Ideally, the important person will take note your existence and, in a perfect world, will ask you a question or in some way give you an opening to continue to talk with them. If that happens, in your next comment(s) you will want to say something to that important person…

- that they haven't heard before which makes them think; or
- that makes them laugh; or
- ideally, both.

The important person will now see you as an individual—Jeff Jones from marketing—and you have succeeded in creating an opening for yourself for possible future connection to this important person. How you present yourself is as important as what you say. You should speak clearly, confidently and with an upbeat, friendly tone—and you should try to look the person in the eye as you speak.

What can you say? You will need to think fast, but you can prepare for this possibility too. For example, if there has been a recent company-wide meeting, you could say something that refers back to that event, especially if there was something humorous that happened there. Or you can make small talk about the local sports team or even the weather. It really doesn't matter that much what you say, what matters is that you are friendly and confident, though of course deferential and polite.

Don't prolong the moment unnecessarily, and follow their lead in smoothly disengaging and going back to your work. At some point after this encounter you will hopefully have an opportunity to re-introduce yourself to that important person and, perhaps, have a chance to volunteer for an assignment or be considered for a promotion.

Evolving Your Narratives

Throughout your life you will continue to develop your skills, your narratives, and your personal outreach strategies. As you develop a suite of ways to talk about yourself to different people and in varied contexts, you will learn to modify your talking points, omitting some and using others to fit the situation. Self-presentation is a nuanced skill, one that professionals are always shaping and developing throughout their careers.

Step Four: Find Your Niche in the Opportunity Ecosystem

Every job and career option is embedded in a larger world. Think of the people and companies that interest you as being part of an *ecosystem*, which is defined as "a community of organisms interacting with the environment around them." The professional ecosystems you care about are *industries* that include people and organizations that are already related to one another in some way. *Industry* is a broad term that can include commercial businesses + the government agencies that regulate them + the nonprofit organizations that study and monitor them. There will be serendipitous overlaps between one set of people and another, and there may be multiple professional ecosystems that you are interested in exploring.

Your goal is to be part of the ecosystem(s) so that when opportunities materialize, you will already be known to the decision makers and will be in the mix as they cast around for candidates.

Question: How can you become part of an ecosystem if you don't already have a job in one of those companies?

Answer: This is one of the most important insights to take from this Guide: you become part of the world you wish to join by communicating with the people you find there.

Question: What will you communicate about when you connect with new people?

Answer: You will communicate about yourself, your skills, and your interest in — and knowledge of — their world. You will ask good, thoughtful questions that will encourage people to be interested in your approach to the issues they care about.

Question: Why should they care about you?

Answer: Well, they won't always care about you, but over time, some people will care and will respond to your interest. If you assume you are welcome in the world you seek to join, and are welcoming to others, you will find your people, grow your network and begin to occupy a niche in that ecosystem.

Your ultimate goal through networking is to get in a position to talk to the people who are already doing the work that interests you. You want to ask them how they got there, what they consider important, and what they think their biggest challenges are, so that you can learn how to add value in that world—how you can help them—and get hired to think about the things that interest *you.*

Becoming part of the ecosystem means positioning yourself to be considered for a job before it gets advertised, even before the organization realizes it needs to fill that role. As much as you can, you want to be known to the companies, professional organizations and people who are doing the work that interests you. You want to be *networked to them* so that when they do have an opportunity to grow their staff, they think of you!

Networking is the most important strategy to master if you want to find exciting job opportunities and create a rich and substantial career over your lifetime.

Networking Like a Pro

With the Internet, you have extraordinary access to a wealth of information that can help you find and cultivate the contacts you need to find the job you want. But how do you network with people you don't know? Well, like anything worth doing, networking is worth doing well, and if you follow the steps outlined below, you will quickly become a networking pro!

Some people are intimidated by networking, while others seem to have an instinctive feeling for building their social and professional networks. Whichever side of that divide you are on, *you definitely can develop and enhance your networking skills over time*. It can be a little scary to realize that there are no more "traditional" career paths to count on, and one way to defeat that fear is to **embrace networking as a strategy for strengthening your resilience in the face of uncertainty**.

In my experience, to get over the fear of networking it helps to:
- give yourself permission to start with small steps,
- practice writing short, friendly outreach emails,
- don't let negative responses or being ignored defeat you,
- push yourself to step outside your comfort zone as often as you can, and
- remind yourself that anyone you meet—no matter how accomplished they may be—has their own fears and insecurities.

As you begin to reach out and connect with others, you will simply become less fearful of networking. By prioritizing actually meeting others in person, you will develop more and more real world professional contacts. And having more relationships will help you create a robust network of individuals who know you, who care about you and who can, possibly, help you over the long term.

Social media turns out to be incredibly useful to help reduce barriers to connecting with people, and truly effective networking in the 21st century relies on communication across all possible channels and platforms. Remember that you are playing a long game, so creating and maintaining loose ties with a lot of different people will be very useful in support of your career efforts over your lifetime.

To get started, you need to
- reach out to people you already know, and
- take the initiative to meet people you don't know.

Together, these two simple strategies will help you grow your professional network.

Each time you reach out to meet with someone in this process, you are asking for an *"informational interview"*—you are *not* asking for a job.

In an *informational interview*, (also referred to as an "information interview") you are seeking to *meet new people* and *learn about their careers* and their interests.

As the conversation progresses, *ask them for* **ideas, suggestions and referrals**. You should also be sharing with them what you think you are good at, what interests you and what you believe you can contribute to the organizations and industries you are interested in learning more about.

Ideally, you should leave every informational interview with at least one new person to contact. **Be sure to create and update a spreadsheet to keep track of all these new people and organizations**.

Game Plan to Reach Out Through Your Inner Circle

Start by looking at the people closest to you—your family, friends, professors and mentors. This is your inner circle. The people they will refer you to become your second circle, and then as you network outwards, you build more and more circles of overlapping connections.

Ask your inner circle for *ideas, suggestions and referrals* to people they may know who might be able to help you as you search for the next great opportunity. Some of your inner circle folks may only know you slightly—or may have known you when you were younger, so you need to help them by sharing your career interests as well as possible companies and organizations where you'd like to work.

Use your draft narratives about who you are and what you are interested in. Ask these close family and mentors for general feedback on your self-presentation as well as for specific ideas, suggestions and referrals.

Next, expand your world by reaching out to people you don't know. Start with the people your inner circle will connect with you.

Golden Tip #7
Build Your Own Personal Social Capital.
As you grow your professional network, your challenge will be to leverage these contacts. Don't underestimate the power of weak or loose ties. Build your own *personal social capital* by continuously investing time and attention in socializing and networking.

Golden Tip #8
ABC = Always Be Connecting.

There is no substitute for face-to-face socializing when it comes to creating professional options, because your next opportunity can emerge directly or indirectly from someone you meet at an event. You invest in yourself every time you exchange contact information with someone new.

Be respectful of their relationship with your original connection:

■ While you should assume that anything you say *might* get back to your inner circle supporter, don't assume that the new contact will definitely reach back and tell your supporter that they've met you.

■ You *absolutely must* tell your supporter if you meet with someone they connected you to, so they can reach out to their contact to thank *them* for taking the time to meet or talk with you.

Remember: your inner circle supporter asked someone to do them a favor by meeting or talking with you. If your supporter never finds out about your meeting, they won't get the chance to thank their contact directly.

As time passes, continue to check in with those who have helped you — they are part of your career world now, invested to some degree in your success. Be sure to thank whoever helps you get a call or meeting with someone they suggest. They may be able to help you again in the future, plus you may be able to help them, too. Remember: *what goes around comes around*, and maintaining your connections over time will help you build social capital.

Continuously build out your circles of contacts and acquaintances. Often it is not the people closest to us who are the most helpful, but rather the people we are connected to indirectly. Never underestimate the power of weak or loose ties as you continue to develop your networks. Don't forget to be proactive in serving as a networking resource for others, and remember to update your contacts with periodic check-ins. You can share resources (like articles,) let people know if you change jobs, and keep up with their career and life changes as well. See **Chapter Two** for more detail on using Social Media to maintain your professional networks.

Game Plan to Reach Out to Strangers

The next step is to expand your network even more by reaching out to people and companies where you lack any obvious connection. Here is a game plan—and remember to keep track of what you are doing on your Excel spreadsheet!

- Do some research online and find ten (or more) people or companies that do the exact thing (or something close) that interests you.
- Work with your career services office to identify alumni of your college who have made careers in the field you are interested in—and include them in your list too.
- Study the people on your list and note what they have done in their careers—what degrees they've earned, what job roles they've had, what companies or groups they've been associated with either as an employee or as a volunteer. What skills do they use? Start developing those skills, and learning as much as you can about those people and those groups or companies.
- Strategize how you will reach out to the people on your list. For alumni, you usually can reach out by email or through LinkedIn. For people you don't have an obvious connection to, consider the following steps:
  - Find a conference where they will be on a panel and go up to them—maybe use social media or email to reach them ahead of time—introduce yourself and tell them about your dream for yourself. Ask them questions. Offer to intern for them (if you can.)
  - Go to events and conferences and immerse yourself in the world you want to join. Don't be intimidated—think creatively about how to connect with the people you want to meet.
  - Do some research on the challenges facing the companies or industries and try to develop some new approaches to their problems; consider building a portfolio of your work and share it online.
  - Seek out like-minded people in clubs and professional organizations and continually expand your network. Be aware that many professional organizations will offer student rates as well as access to job postings.

**Golden Tip #9
Practice Small Talk
with Strangers.**

Use any opportunities that present themselves to you to hone your small talk skills. Practice chatting people up on the line at the grocery store, on the bus, or in a waiting room. Smile, try to engage and be prepared to be rebuffed a few times—the times when you do get a positive response will more than make up for the times when people are not interested in talking with you.

Writing Short Friendly Outreach Emails

Practice writing short friendly outreach emails that will introduce you to strangers and encourage the recipient to respond to you. The content of the email is similar to the first paragraph of a cover letter when you apply for a job, and it should inspire the reader to reach back out to you.

Start your email with a standard greeting, such as Dear Mr. Jones—note, not Dear Mr. John Jones. Even when the connection is personal, such as a family referral, you should err on the side of being a little more formal when you reach out professionally.

Here is a sample outreach email to someone you met at a family event:

Dear Mr. Jones:

As I hope you may recall, we were briefly introduced at the backyard party held last week at my aunt Tillie's home. I am a senior at State College where I majored in Communications, and I am writing to follow up on your kind offer to help me identify possible job opportunities in the public relations field. Would it be possible for me to call you sometime next week? Please let me know some dates and times when we could speak by phone. I could also come to your office if that would be convenient for you.

Thank you for your consideration and I look forward to speaking with you soon.

Sincerely,

Annie Smith

Here is a sample email to someone you are not connected to:

Dear Mr. Jones:

As a recent graduate of State College, where I majored in Communications, I am extremely interested in pursuing a career in Public Relations. I really appreciated reading your recent comment on the blog "Today's PR Executive" where you said that the field is changing rapidly as social media is transforming how consumers relate to company brands.

I read in Ad Age that your firm was recently selected by Spotify to help with their digital branding. I am a huge Spotify fan, and was an intern for them last summer. I believe that my educational background, my Spotify connections and my strong desire to work in public relations will enable me to make a strong contribution to your efforts.

Would it be possible for us to speak briefly by phone or meet in person sometime in the next two weeks? Even if your firm doesn't have an opening for me, I'd be happy to share what I know about Spotify with you, and perhaps you can give me some advice as I start my career in public relations.

Thank you for your consideration and I look forward to hearing from you.

Sincerely,

Annie Smith

Business Cards

Even if you are still a student or not fully employed, you can and should have a business card to hand out when you meet new people. Many schools will offer business card printing for students through their career services offices. Or you can print your own cards at Fedex. Either way, be sure that the card is conservative, professional and appropriate. You should establish a new email address for professional networking, one that is simple and non-cutesy (do not use "cheeky1@gmail, etc.) If you are not sure how the information on the card should be laid out, ask for help from career services or look at business card samples.

For networking purposes, you do not need to include your personal home address—just your name, your email, and your phone number will be sufficient. Many students will include their school's name and seal, and may include a line that states their expected graduation date and major. Some people include their LinkedIn profile URL on their card, especially if they have a common last name.

Introducing Yourself at Networking Parties and Events

As you become more confident, you will learn to enter networking gatherings on your own and find new people who will talk with you. This is not as hard as it seems, and it will get easier over time. There are many strategies for success at networking events, including chatting people up at the bar or food table and joining groups. It may seem easier to join larger groups (3 or more people) but you really can walk up to anyone at the event. Every person there is open to meeting new people and will likely offer you a smile and a greeting.

When you approach a person who is standing on their own, you smile, say Hi, say your name and then *stop speaking* and wait to let the other person reply. You should listen to what they say (usually their name and maybe the name of their firm) and then you can follow up with small talk such as "It's my first time at this event, and I am impressed with the turnout—how about you? Have you been to these things before?" Try to keep the conversation going for a few minutes, sharing something about yourself and asking them something about themselves.

The point of the conversation is to learn something about the other person and share something about yourself with them—besides your business card.

When you enter a space where there is a networking event, take a look around for groups of people who appear friendly and welcoming. Pick a group and walk over to them and listen for a while. It's important to listen before you speak so that when you do join the conversation, you can make a comment or ask a question that is relevant.

Making Yourself Memorable

How can you make yourself more memorable to the people you meet? After all, your goal when networking is to weave threads of connection between you and the new people you are meeting. Ideally, you want the other person to remember you well when you reach out — or even, for them to reach out to you. The objective is not to gather as many business cards as possible, but to make one or more real connections that could lead to another more in–depth conversation. A good friend of mine tells a story about when he was a young professional, his boss would take him to events — and if he came away from the event with just one business card of someone he really connected with, that was considered a success by his boss.

There are many dimensions to the idea of **Emotional Intelligence**, and I will return to this idea several times in the Guide. For general purposes, *Emotional Intelligence* is a capacity to "recognize one's own and other people's emotions, appropriately recognize and label feelings, guide thinking and behavior and manage/adjust emotions to adapt to environments or achieve one's goals." We may demonstrate *Emotional Intelligence* through our actions, and those who do so are potentially more likely to be recalled positively by others.

Here is a short list of *emotionally intelligent actions* you can take when introducing yourself to a person for the first time. They won't necessarily make the person remember you, but they will help make them *like* you — which is the first step toward being memorable!

- Smile and show genuine (not fake) enthusiasm in your conversation.
- Be friendly, make direct eye contact and offer a firm handshake if you can.
- Ask open-ended questions like "how did you get into that?" or "what is your favorite part of doing that?"
- Ask how you can help them — networking is best when it's a two way street.

- Listen to the answers. Ask a brief follow up question—and listen to that answer too! Stay in the moment with the person and try to avoid using half your brain to figure out what you are going to say next.

- Use the person's name in a sentence when you are closing the conversation and immediately take a moment to memorize something about them. This is as easy as "Thanks for chatting with me Joseph, let's be in touch" or "So nice to meet you Jill, hope you enjoy the rest of the conference."

- This sort of outreach may seem like it will be hard, but over time, I promise, it will get easier. Be yourself, be genuine. People will generally respond positively to authentic expressions of interest, and the more prepared you are for the interactions, the better. If you believe in yourself and step out of your comfort zone, you will be surprised at the good things that can happen.

Golden Tip #10
Build Your Personal
Board of Directors.
Find people willing to guide you in the future by being authentic and hard working in the present.

A Personal Board of Directors:
The Secret of Successful People

One of the secrets to success is having a team of people who are interested in your success and who can give you smart, helpful feedback when you need work advice.

Some people are born into families where their parents or relatives—who are in business or are professionals of some sort—can serve as their career advisors, but many people do not have family they can turn to for business and career advice. Your "personal board of directors" can help you by serving as a sounding board for career challenges and decisions.

As you finish school and start working, start looking around for people who might be good advisors for you—and seek their advice. Take them to coffee or lunch, ask them about their careers, and explain your career aspirations. Over time, if they are interested in you and willing to continue to engage with you, be sure to cultivate those relationships.

By the way, this is an informal thing, and not something you label or put on a resume—though you may describe a former colleague or former boss as a "mentor" to you.

Even if you do have family to talk to, getting an outside perspective can often be really helpful and eye opening. While an outsider may not love you the way a family member might, an outside mentor can compare you and your career to others who are similarly situated. A mentor can give you advice that reflects their experience, advice that might be different from what your parents will tell you.

Creating Your Professional Reputation

What is a reputation? It's the opinion of the world, about you, your character and your achievements. Of course, most of the world has no idea that you exist and, as mentioned earlier, doesn't care at all if you succeed or fail. So your reputation is something that matters greatly to you, but far less to other people—and yet the opinions of some of those people matter and will define your reputation.

Thanks to our digital technology, the world has grown both larger and smaller in ways that present opportunities for—and risks to—your professional and personal reputations. The next Chapter offers strategies for managing your use of social media as you begin to develop your professional reputation in the digital world, recognizing that most people have an already established online existence that pre-dates their college years.

But there is more to developing a professional reputation than just managing your digital presence. For example, research scientists and academics build their reputations by doing research and publishing peer reviewed, original work. In every field, there will always be opportunities to publish new ideas as well as analyses and critiques of conventional wisdom.

Golden Tip #11
Safeguard Your Reputation.
Think about the impacts of your words and actions BEFORE you speak or act. Here are two examples of the advice of sages, old and new:

- "Regard your good name as the richest jewel you possess—for credit is like fire; when once you have kindled it you may easily preserve is, but if you once extinguish it, you will find it an arduous task to rekindle it again. The way to gain a good reputation is to endeavor to be what you desire to appear."
—Socrates (469 BC–399 BC)
- "It takes 20 years to build a reputation and five minutes to ruin it. If you think about that, you'll do things differently."
—Warren Buffet

The tried and true methods of reputation building are…networking, networking, and networking, plus **doing your best work in whatever position you have so that those who hear about your efforts hear only good things about you.**

To build your reputation in your field,

- Do good work, no matter what the assignment.
- Join and find ways to participate in professional organizations.
- Go to conferences and conventions and introduce yourself to others.
- Offer to moderate a panel, or make a presentation at a conference.
- Blog, publish, and find opportunities to speak in public.

In addition to taking steps to build your *professional* recognition, there are things you can do to create and enhance your *personal* reputation.

To build your personal reputation in your community,

- Join alumni groups and go to the social events.
- Volunteer for your school as an alumni interviewer.
- Join groups and organizations doing social service and community building.
- Seek out opportunities to work on task forces in your community, volunteer for local nonprofits, maybe serve on a board of directors—even a residents' committee in your apartment building can be a good place to meet people.

These days, it is more important than ever to cultivate personal real world connections. The obvious downside of the Internet is that there are many more people applying for every open position and for you to succeed, you will need to deploy every marketing strategy available to you.

Ask the people you meet in your community about their work and what advice they might have for you—even if they work in completely different fields. Be open and continually seek to expand your world and meet new people.

Building your reputation is a long game, but even in the short term, every new person you cultivate is a person who will begin to develop an opinion of you. Over time, the cumulative impact of all these encounters will be like money in the bank—positive social capital—for your reputation.

Finally, it is also the case that in many parts of the world, the Internet is not easily or reliably accessed, so these techniques and strategies for marketing yourself "offline" and developing your professional reputation will continue to be critical to career development in those environments.

Chapter One Take Aways

1. **Explore your interests, strengths and options.** Use the assessment tools and other resources in your college career office.
2. **Be Intentional. Don't drift along!** Challenge yourself and always seek out new opportunities to learn skills and meet new people.
3. **Be Brave and Be Persistent.** Take small steps every day and every week to boost your confidence and gain experience.
4. **Be Prepared and Be Alert.** Keep up with the news generally, and also be an avid reader of blogs, websites and professional publications that cover your topics of interest.
5. **Network, Network, Network.** Meet new people, ask questions, be open and friendly.

Golden Tip #12
Read, Read, Read.
Read widely in the professional journals in the fields you are interested in, keep up with relevant websites and blogs (does your professor write one?) and have some idea of what is happening in the world. Do not rely on television for your news.

2 | Thriving in a Social Media World

Life In the Digital Age

Before the Internet existed, people built their personal social capital and developed their professional reputations much more slowly. These days, there is hardly anyone who doesn't already have one or more online *personas*, which are creating reputational waves just by existing in the virtual world.

Indeed, the Internet has so completely changed the way that we live in the real world that it no longer even makes any sense to think of the virtual world and the real world as distinct spheres. Since interacting with technology is part of everyone's daily existence, our communications in the virtual world might as well be considered part of our real world.

What does this mean for you as you look for a job and develop your career over time?

- You will need to actively manage your online and offline reputation with care, and
- You will need to find ways to "brand yourself" online —which is another way of saying you need to distinguish yourself from the crowd.

In addition to the advice offered in this Guide, there are many books and articles focusing on how to brand yourself– see the **Resource File: Additional Reading** for some suggestions.

The most important thing to keep in mind as you go forward is that there are *reputational dangers* associated with social media and all digital interactions, and you need to be vigilant and pro-active when it comes to your reputation. It is famously said that a reputation, once lost, is nearly impossible to recover. While that is a harsh message, it is worth taking to heart early in your career so that you can avoid being professionally disappointed later.

Note that if you are already employed, you should **be sure to read and be familiar with your employer's social media policy**, if they have one. See **Chapter Five** for a discussion of smart, cautious approaches to the use of social media at work. For example, some people who post comments to Twitter or other sites have a "disclaimer" that they include in their profile, saying that their comments "are their own and do not represent the views of their employer." It is not clear if such disclaimers would protect you legally if your employer objects to the comments.

This Chapter offers basic steps that you should already be taking to ensure that your reputation — starting with your online presence — is positive and will enhance your chances of being hired to do the interesting and challenging work you deserve.

Incidentally, I hope it goes without saying that no one should ever — ever — be sending any photos of a sexual nature to anyone else using their mobile phone or computer — *no sexting*!

One: Honestly Inventory Your Online Presence

If you have ever posted anything on any site — such as Facebook, Twitter, LinkedIn, Instagram, Pinterest, Reddit, Weibo or YouTube — or in the comments section of a blog or website — then you have already begun to reveal yourself to potential employers. What will they see?

Do you use alternate names, aliases, handles or personas on different sites? For example, do you have a particular user name for when you play video games with other people? Many people used different screen names when they were younger, and employers may link you and your previous aliases when they do reputation searches prior to making an offer of employment.

- **Google yourself *and your aliases*** and immediately start to take steps to take down/delete/remove anything that is possibly ***unprofessional.***
- *Before you do your search, log out of Google and use a different browser than you usually use with Google, or search in Incognito (Chrome) or Private (Firefox) mode so that your search result will be **as unfiltered as possible** by the algorithms Google has tailored for you.*
- *Do a search for **images of yourself** and make sure that no one has usurped your image for their own activity.*
- *Set up a **Google news alert** for your name and variations on your name, so that you can keep yourself informed about both positive and negative reputational developments.*

Make sure you see what others are seeing about you!

Unprofessional is a big category, and includes everything from misspellings and bad grammar to any signs of inappropriate behavior or prejudicial attitudes. Employers are looking for evidence of ***bad judgment***—including signs of alcohol and drug use such as photos of you at parties looking wasted, or comments in an Instagram or Twitter feed about "partying all night."

Bad judgment extends to possibly inadvertent discrepancies between your resume and easily available online information posted in your profiles. Take a good close look at the profiles you have on any and all sites, and, wearing a potential employer's hat, make sure that you like what you see. Are the job titles, activities, hobbies, interests and *likes* consistent across different platforms? Your profiles don't have to be identical, but if one site profile lists you as a country music super fan, and on another you say you hate country music and love to go to all night raves and dance to techno, that will raise a red flag for most reviewers.

Employers are looking for creative, trustworthy and hardworking individuals. You can and should use the online world to project that—hopefully accurate!—image of yourself. *Think carefully about how you are demonstrating your skill set and your personality to potential employers through your online presence.*

- Are you expressing yourself clearly, correctly and consistently?
- Do you include (post) examples of recent creative work that you have done?
- Would a review of your recent online interactions show that you are a thoughtful person and that you get along with others?

In today's world, it is essentially not possible to take total control of your online presence, since there are myriad ways that we leave digital tracks as we shop, socialize and live online. What people will see about you online is constantly evolving as you live your life, however, it is possible to be intentional and thoughtful about your own communications, and that is the first place to start. See **Clean Up Your Digital Footprint**, below, for more detailed suggestions.

Two: Revisit Your Privacy Settings For All Sites

Wherever you have an online presence that includes a profile or other way to control your engagement with the site or service, take the time to review your privacy settings. *Your goal is to ensure that the privacy settings maximize your privacy while still enabling potential employers to find you.*

Facebook: Many people set up their Facebook or other accounts when they were younger, and may not have updated their privacy settings. Since Facebook is where people tend to be most personal, be sure your settings are working for you and not against you. For example, **the default setting in Facebook makes all your posts public**—so be sure that you specifically select in the privacy settings so that only your friends can see your posts.

If you are a member of different **Facebook Groups**, it is likely that not everyone in each of those groups is a friend of yours. Be aware that Facebook maintains an *activity tracker* that keeps track of all your *likes*, views, *clicks* and comments—and anyone—friend or not—who has access to you through a Facebook Group can take a screenshot of your activity.

Similarly, **Twitter** tracks your *likes* and anyone who looks at your profile on Twitter can click through to see your likes and take a screenshot of them. They don't have to be a follower of yours, and you won't be notified that this happened.

For your own safety, it's a good idea to keep the **Geotagging** function in your phone—and within the apps you use—turned off except when you want it on so that a taxi can find you.

Be aware that search engines maintain search histories, and while most prospective employers will not be able to access those (since they would need your passwords or a search warrant) it's still a good idea to regularly wipe out your own search history. See discussion on the use of an employer's computers in **Chapter Five**.

Better safe than sorry is the best advice in this situation. If an employer decides to pass on your employment application, you will never know the reason—so make sure that you are not inadvertently sabotaging yourself with a damaging digital trail.

Three: Enhance Your Personal Brand

These days, obviously, the resume and cover letter you send are not the only things an employer will see about you. All major employers—and most smaller ones as well—will take the time to review job-seekers' online presence. You need to be vigilant about what they will see and practice good online "personal brand management."

At the same time, you do want to make your profile available for recruiters to come upon in their keyword searches. So there is a balance to strike between how much you want to reveal to the world—and potential identity thieves—and how much control you can exert over your digital identity.

There are **both defensive and pro-active steps** you can take, always remembering that *you are the one deciding when to go online and when to take a break from personal promotion efforts.* There is a time to network and promote yourself, and a time to turn to non-career stuff, including investing time and energy in friendships and new adventures.

Try to be sensitive to yourself and give yourself time off from online activities when you need it. See **Chapter Five** for more on self care strategies and remember that building a reputation and a career is something you will do over your lifetime—it's a marathon, not a sprint.

Key Defensive Steps to Take

Clean Up Your Digital Footprint

After your initial inventory of your online presence, you need to *take the steps necessary to actually clean up your digital footprint*. If you don't know how to remove something from a site, ask for help from your friends or search online for instructions. For many people who have had Facebook accounts from an early age, there may be quite a lot of material to review and possibly remove.

Don't panic, but don't ignore that iceberg of potentially self-sabotaging material. Depending on how active you were online as a younger person, reliable experts have estimated that it can take about 2–4 hours to review and remove about 5 years of historical material.

Remove anything from any site that you have posted—or allowed others to post—that detracts from the impression you want employers to have about you. This includes comments on Facebook as well as any reviews you have posted on Amazon or Yelp or YouTube or other sites you visit.

Develop a list of adjectives you hope employers will think of when they think of you—and use it as a checklist when you consider whether to remove a photo or text message from a site. When appropriate, use the words themselves to describe yourself. What do you think they are looking for in new employees? Smart? Creative? Trustworthy? Professional? Reliable? Collaborative? What else might employers seek in a new hire? Make sure that when employers look at you online, those preferred words are the adjectives that your online presence brings to mind.

Monitor and continually manage your footprint so that the world sees what you want them to see when your name is mentioned. You want to ensure that employers see positive rather than unflattering information about you, which may suggest closing down old social media accounts.

Consider using a service like Rep'nUp to clean up your footprint.

Perhaps the main strategy for overcoming bad content that you cannot remove from the Internet is to *increase* the amount of material that is circulating about you. Making the effort to enhance your digital presence is a good idea whether or not you are trying to bury unattractive content, and the social media outreach activities discussed throughout the Guide will help you create positive content.

However, even as you create good content for people to find when they search your name, if you have a lot of old, bad content out there, you may wish to take additional steps to remove it, detailed next.

Remove Third Party Content

If your search turns up anything negative about you, or you have been publicly attacked or shamed on a website, you can and should make an effort to remove this content from search results.

You can send Google a take down request, based on a copyright violation if there is one. Search "take down request" on Google's home page for support [support.google.com] for instructions on how to proceed.

De-Index Social Accounts

You can take advantage of the capability that many sites offer to "de-index" your profiles. This means you can tell the site (eg Facebook, LinkedIn, etc) that you do NOT want the profile of you that is on their site to appear in a Google search. Each provider has different steps to take to accomplish this, but if you take the time to do this, your social media profiles on these sites will not be available to strangers doing searches of your name. Remember, when you are looking for a job you may wish to keep some profiles available, like LinkedIn, so de-indexing is a step to take only if you really want to disappear from the online world.

In addition to making the request for de-indexing on the social media sites, you can also work directly with Google through their "webmasters" pages: www.google.com/webmasters

Delete Some Accounts

If you have a profile on an account that you no longer regularly access or need, you should consider deleting it. However, remember that some sites don't really delete your profile when you tell them to do so—they just "soft delete" which means they keep the profile on their server but block others from seeing the information.

To protect yourself no matter whether the profile is deleted or not, before you ask for the delete, go ahead and edit the profile down as much as you can. Try to eliminate all unflattering information and all easily identifiable data points (birthdate, gender, address, etc.)

Some sites make it hard to find the delete button—but you can do a Google search "How can I delete my account in website X" and you should be able to get instructions. If you need to, you can contact customer service.

There is a lot of valuable information about deleting accounts at www.backgroundchecks.org/justdeleteme/ and there are commercial services which can help you, such as www.accountkiller.com.

Key Proactive Steps To Take

Finish/Complete all Profiles

Wherever you have an online profile, be sure you complete the profile carefully and comprehensively. In the US and Europe, **LinkedIn** is such an important networking tool that it makes sense to learn as much as you can about how to maximize your use of the site. There are many publications in-print and online that offer LinkedIn advice, and on the LinkedIn site there are links to helpful tutorials. Use them!

Use Keywords! For each section of every profile, you have a chance to sell yourself, so be sure to include any and all keywords that may be related to various jobs and industries that interest you. Remember a computer algorithm—not a person—will search the sites and the employer will only find you if the words in your profile match the words in a job description. Use keywords from the profiles of people who have the job(s) that you want. In this case, copying keywords from what others have included in their profiles is OK.

Make sure your word choice is appropriate and professional; make sure you include material that augments your profile professionally, and make sure you regularly update your profiles so they offer a current picture of your activities, skills and strengths.

Post an appropriate, attractive headshot. The headshot should be of your head and maybe your shoulders but nothing else. Dress nicely, make sure your hair is neat and professional, use make-up conservatively, and smile!

Actively build your professional profile. Ask co-workers to recommend you on LinkedIn well before you decide to leave a job, and offer to do the same for them.

> **Golden Tip #13**
> **Influence What Employers See About You Online.**
> Make a checklist of the adjectives you want employers to think of when they review you as a potential hire, use those words yourself when appropriate, and post things that will inspire others to use those words to describe you.

When you update a profile on LinkedIn, consider carefully whether you need to notify all your contacts at that moment. Sometimes you just want to add to your profile without making a big announcement to everyone you know. There is a special setting in LinkedIn that controls who is notified when you make changes.

Regularly revisit and *update the profiles* you have on all sites—and don't forget alumni databases.

Market Yourself Online

Enhancing your presence online means more than merely making sure that employers will not find potentially damaging information about you. You need to pro-actively enhance your online reputation by deliberately building and expanding your online presence with positive material. As noted earlier, this is a good idea on its own, and it can help combat any negative material that may be out there.

You are *deliberately curating your digital identity*, keeping in mind that there is an extraordinary amount of online material that is out of your control, and that the technology and how to use it is always evolving rapidly.

You are essentially pursuing an ongoing personal social media campaign, sometimes in stealth mode and sometimes, when you have the reasons to do it, in an overt mode—but always with careful, deliberate intentionality.

You don't always have to be super active on social media, and in fact it's a good idea to step back frequently to assess what you are doing, how it makes you feel, and what you are achieving with your efforts. Sometimes it's better to stay away from the virtual world, knowing you can always return to it when you have something you want to share with others. See **Chapters Five and Six** for suggestions about work/life integration and balance.

Golden Tip #14
Copying Others is OK When It Comes to Keywords.
When you are completing an online profile you want to use a lot of keywords so that computer algorithms used by employers and recruiters will find you. Copy the keywords used by those who have the job(s) you want!

When you do go online, here are some tips:

- Develop a consistent voice in all your online activity.
- Use appropriate, attractive, professional images on all sites
- Join discussion groups that are topic specific on sites like LinkedIn or Facebook and contribute professionally phrased comments.
- Post resources like links to articles that are relevant to the discussion topics, and if you have published on a topic, link to your own work!
- Use social media to expand your professional network by "liking" posts of others, following others, and reaching out when you can to turn online connections into real world friendships.

In 2017, the main platforms to use for professional recognition are LinkedIn, Facebook and Twitter, with Instagram, Pinterest and You Tube coming up fast. There are also already more than 100 million blogs, as well as personal websites where people showcase their work; of course, the specific techniques and platforms to use for professional outreach and recognition will change over time.

When you do this effectively, you will turn your online presence into an effective *selling strategy* that will work for you throughout your professional life. Yes, I said a selling strategy because that is what all resumes are for—and *the Internet is now your resume*. Making the Internet work for you will be an ongoing and critical part of your career strategy for the rest of your life.

Chapter Two Take-Aways

There are **reputational dangers** associated with social media and all digital interactions, and you need to be vigilant and pro-active when it comes to your reputation.

1. **No sexting!**
2. **No sexting!**

3 | Presenting Your Best Self

Getting in the Game

The hockey player Wayne Gretzky famously said, "You miss 100% of the shots you don't take"—and the same advice applies to your career. You have to get in the game, and apply for opportunities where you can make a credible argument that you are qualified. I tell people that "you can't turn down what hasn't been offered." People constantly talk themselves out of applying for perfectly possible jobs and school programs, rationalizing that they won't get in or won't get picked.

You need to be pro-active about opportunity. There is no reason not to apply for positions or school programs, since you never know what might happen. For one thing, you do not know what the pool of applicants looks like for any job or school at the exact moment you are applying, and for another, you may have just the right mix of qualifications and connections to be chosen. You can do things to increase your chances of being selected for a job or admitted to a graduate program, but only if you make the initial decision to apply.

The overall message of this Guide is that you will create a world of opportunity for yourself by implementing personal best practices that thicken your social and professional ties. It is still the case, however, especially when you are starting out, that you need to identify opportunities worth applying for, and quickly send your tailored cover letter and resume so that you will be a competitive applicant.

Golden Tip #15
You Can't Turn Down What Hasn't Been Offered.
You have to get in the game, and pro-actively seek out opportunities that you are qualified for and interested in. Don't spend time worrying and deciding that you won't get picked and talk yourself out of applying.

In this Chapter we will look at

- Strategies for efficiently identifying opportunities worth applying for,
- Action steps and advice for superior resume, cover and thank you letter writing,
- Tips for acing interviews and increasing your chances of being chosen, and
- Suggestions for how to think about additional credentials.

Finding Opportunities

In **Chapter Four** there is a detailed discussion of how to overcome obstacles to getting hired, which complements this overview of job search strategies.

- Most broadly, *you can search* Internet job boards by job titles and location. For example, you can search and create alerts in general job aggregators like Indeed, or LinkedIn, or you can search in specialized aggregators like Idealist or government job boards. In **Resource File: Internet Resources** you will find some job boards and websites to get started. Remember that in this type of searching, *varying your keywords* will produce a wider range of results.
- *You can narrow your search* process by going to the websites of particular companies and reviewing their open positions. Some companies will let you upload a resume and if/when their algorithm matches you to an open position, they will alert you so that you can decide if you want to apply. It is also a good idea to continue to continue to check your school's job posting system, as many entry-level positions will remain of interest to you in your early twenties.
- *You can explore your social media network* to identify people and companies that interest you. For example, using filters such as *alumni of your school*, you can search in LinkedIn for people working in particular cities, companies or industries. If you follow the trail from an alum's profile to a company that they worked at in the past, you will learn more about their career path and possibly find interesting career options for yourself.

■ *You can reach out for informational interviews* to people you identify through your inner and secondary circles, and as you continuously meet new people, remember to keep track of their affiliations and referrals on your Excel tracking spreadsheet. Over time, the spreadsheet will fill up with websites of interesting companies that you can explore when you have time — and if you find an opening, you can circle back to your contact for advice and a possible internal referral.

The right combination of networking and applying to opportunities online will depend on where you are in your career, however according to most experts, **applying online to postings you find on job boards or company websites is only successful around 5% of the time**... so you definitely do not want to spend more than 5–10% of your available job hunting time sitting at your computer applying to job postings!

Plan to allocate as much as 90% of your career development time to networking, reading and investigating new ideas and organizations.

Selling Yourself to Others

In the last chapter we talked about how the Internet is effectively your resume now, so you need to constantly curate your digital identity with your professional reputation in mind. At the same time, you need to create a short resume that you can send with a tailored cover letter when you apply to positions that you see posted.

The use of the Internet and social media in job searching and networking is evolving very rapidly along with changes to the technologies themselves. *What will never change is how human beings actually connect and make meaningful decisions about who to hire and who to fire.* Getting past the human and electronic gatekeepers is harder than ever, so you do need to be constantly revising and improving your personal outreach language.

Golden Tip #16
Use your Minutes.

You may feel that your time is constrained by school, family and/or work commitments, and you may imagine that you are never free to "do what you want to do," but it is almost surely the case that you can control some portion of your time. *Be intentional and make good choices with those minutes, however few they may seem to be!* Over time, you can accomplish a lot working just a few minutes a day or week on a project or an idea. You can always learn something new — even something that seems insurmountably hard — if you break it into steps and apply yourself diligently over time.

The purpose of the resume and cover letter is to sell yourself. You want the reader to see something in the material that makes them want to talk to you. That's it: you are just trying to get in the door for a conversation. You can assume that if you are selected for an interview, the employer believes that you have the qualifications—at least on paper—both to be selected and to do the job once hired.

Being identified as *qualified to be selected* for the position means that the decision maker does not think they will face any questions or concerns if they hire you for the role. But being non-objectionable is not enough to be hired: all other things being equal, you will most likely be selected for the job only if you can positively distinguish yourself from the competition *and* impress the interviewer with your "fit" for the position.

Distinguishing yourself starts with how you present yourself in your cover letter and on your resume. It continues with how you present yourself in the interview and in your follow-up to the interview. In addition, it is very important to activate your social and professional network when you apply for a position, so that you can get a referral if you know anyone who knows the decision maker or who works at the company. See **Chapter Four** for advice on getting past gatekeepers and overcoming obstacles to being hired.

Writing a Great Cover Letter or Outreach Email

These days some job applications don't even allow you to include cover letters, but if they do, be sure to take advantage of this opportunity to showcase your writing skills. Be sure to look carefully if you think that a cover letter is NOT allowed—be sure to **double check**—because most systems *will* permit you to upload *supplemental documents*, which usually can include cover letters and references.

As you evolve your narratives about who you are and what interests you for networking purposes, you should also develop short, smart sentences and paragraphs describing your background, interests and transferrable skills.

A good cover letter:

- highlights how your background qualifies you for the position you are seeking, and allows you to demonstrate some familiarity with the challenges the employer is facing. It is not a summary of your resume, though it will include references to one or more skills or employment experiences you have had.
- is short—one page—to demonstrate that you can focus and write succinctly, and that you respect the reader's time.
- connects your skills to the needs of the employer as stated in the job description under Responsibilities and Qualifications. You can do this by referencing previous accomplishments that match the "required skills" in the target opportunity, by calling attention to your transferable skills and by offering an illustration of how those skills or experiences prepare you to succeed in the role.

A good cover letter makes the reader want to meet you because they believe, based on your letter, that you know enough about their challenges, and have the appropriate skills, to be useful to them.

Your letter, therefore, should not talk about how the position (or the company) will be helpful to you, but rather the opposite: your goal is to convince the reader that you can and will make a meaningful contribution to their efforts from day one.

Cover Letter Structure

A cover letter is written in the basic business letter format and can be included as an attachment to email, pasted into email itself, or uploaded to a company job application system alongside your resume.

Some companies ask you to create a single document that includes your cover letter AND your resume, in which case be sure that your documents have *fixed page breaks so that they don't run together*!

It is easy and smart to create a personal letterhead for cover letters so that if the cover letter is separated from the resume, the reader can still respond. Be sure that your letterhead:

- Is located within the header or footer on the page to save space
- Matches the font of the cover letter and of the resume
- Includes your name, street address, phone and email

Recipient Address and Greeting

If at all possible, try to get a name to write to so that you can avoid using "To Whom it May Concern" or "To the Hiring Manager" or "To Human Resources." You may not always succeed, however it is worth the effort. Whether or not you have a name, the letter is still formatted like a business letter, not a memo. If you do have a name, the letter is addressed formally: *Dear Mr. Jones* –but take note, *not: Dear Mr. John Jones.*

Content of the Letter

Since this is a short letter, you do not want to waste any space. Write concisely and clearly, addressing in the very first paragraph:

- Why you are writing—you are applying to a position or were referred to the reader by a mutual acquaintance,
- Who you are and what you are doing now, and
- Why you believe you are a good fit for this organization and this position, or, why you hope the reader will meet with you.

This one paragraph may be enough for a networking outreach email, perhaps with a concluding sentence like "Thank you for your consideration and I look forward to hearing from you about speaking by phone or meeting in the next two weeks."

For a job opportunity cover letter, after the opening paragraph, you want to convince the reader that you are a viable candidate who would be an asset to their organization. Your writing should convey your best expression of your skill set as it applies to their stated job responsibilities/candidate qualifications, *ideally in the order in which they have listed them in the job description.*

Of course, to create one or two paragraphs that read fluently, you may need to mention some skills, experiences and credentials in a different order from the job description. Remember that you are not summarizing your resume but instead should be highlighting details you think the reader will find relevant.

You want to convey why you are interested in the position and the organization within a discussion of why you are a good fit for the role. **Again, this is not the place to tell them why *you* would benefit from the job. This is the place to tell them why *they* would benefit from working with you**.

For example, you can say *"I will bring my strong work ethic and experience with creating and managing customer databases to [name of organization] and help the Membership department strengthen its internal reporting and support more effective and targeted outreach efforts."*

Try to tell a story about your experience and your skills that frames you as an obvious candidate for their position. Express in clear terms how you developed your relevant and transferable skills, and note the success you have previously had using those skills. Explain briefly why you care about them/their mission and how you see yourself contributing to their efforts.

In the closing paragraph, be sure to ask for an interview and formally express your thanks for their consideration. See samples, below.

Crafting a Winning Resume

An important thing to remember about your resume is that it is a selling tool that you will *modify for different target positions* and audiences.

Especially for people who have had several short-term internships or volunteer opportunities, it's really important to be thoughtful about which previous jobs to include and which skills and experiences you highlight in your bullets.

Make sure that the resume bullets you use highlight your specific skills and experience that match the skills that the employer is seeking in an applicant. Review the **Resource File: Key Skill Sets** for vocabulary that you can customize to illustrate your personal work experiences and your specific skills.

Another important thing to remember is that you *must optimize your resume for computer/algorithm screening*, which means being very intentional about the format (the layout and the font) as well as the word choices.

You must use keywords that are the *exact same search terms* as appear in the job description—and use them near the top of the resume.

In some countries, the software programs will not recognize standard U.S. formats, so check and optimize your resume for the specific language and culture of your target employer.

A third key thing to keep in mind is that employers will look at your online presence alongside your resume, so be sure there are no discrepancies that make you look bad!

While the different profiles do not have to match each other exactly, and neither do the online profiles have to exactly match your resume, you do want to avoid describing the same position differently in different places.

Specifically, be sure that titles you claim for yourself are consistent, and that any bullets about responsibilities and metrics about achievements are the same across all platforms where a reader might see them.

To be crystal clear: while you *are* creating different versions of your resume/your profile for different audiences, you will use the same vocabulary to describe the same positions. You may vary which previous positions to include, which specific software programs or languages you have experience with, or how you summarize yourself professionally. While you can use different language to describe yourself and your interests in different places, be sure there are no contradictions or inconsistencies.

Remember that applicant tracking software systems search for keywords in your work history to filter out candidates. If you don't have keyword-rich job descriptions for each of your past positions, you may not make it past the initial screening process.

Resume Do's

- Use bullets to draw attention to accomplishments and use them consistently
- Use phrases instead of full sentences to be concise/use less space
- Use active verbs and keywords that match the job description(s)
- Try to include metrics (numbers) whenever you can
- Use an easy-to-read font
- Include your contact information at the top of all pages
- Include your email address + phone number but NOT date of birth
- Leave enough space around and between the text
- Have someone else review your document

Resume Don'ts

- Try to fit so much on the page that it becomes difficult to read—use two pages if necessary
- Use personal pronouns
- Use a font smaller than 10pt
- Forget to check for spelling and grammar mistakes—do not rely on the computer spell check
- List an interest or experience unless you are prepared to talk about it

Comparing a Curriculum Vitae (C.V.) to a Resume

C.V.'s

- several pages long, very descriptive
- used for applying to academic or research positions
- focus on academic, curricular and scholarly accomplishments
- include a complete list of publications

Resumes

- one page is best, two pages if you must
- written with bullet points and phrases
- include work experiences and other information e.g., interests, skills
- used for applying to any type of employment or graduate program

Sample Opportunity:
Entry Level Marketing Assistant

Review the following sample job opportunity, the cover letters, the resumes and the thank you letters of the two candidates, and answer the following questions:

- Which candidate do you think the employer will interview? Perhaps both?
- What factors do you think will distinguish the candidates from each other? Do you think the resumes and cover letters are sufficiently targeted to the job description?
- What questions will the employer be asking and what will be the answers from each candidate?
- Is there any material difference between the two thank you letters?
- Who do you expect would be offered the position?

This exercise should help you think about how you are presenting yourself when you apply for positions, and what steps you could take to distinguish yourself more competitively. There are no right or wrong answers, and every employer will be different. All will be looking for specific skill sets, and some may not even consider applicants without explicit specific technology experience such as Microsoft Office.

As you consider our hypothetical applicants Jill and Annie, think about how each candidate could distinguish herself in an interview. In the end, the employer will chose the candidate who has demonstrated that they meet both the stated qualifications for the position and the unstated "fit" issues discussed in the section on *Job Interviewing Tips and Strategies* that follows below.

STATE COLLEGE JOB OPPORTUNITY POSTING

ABC Communications seeks an entry level Marketing Assistant

Job Summary/General Purpose of Job
The Marketing Assistant will provide administrative support services to an assigned marketing project or work group. The assistant will facilitate customer and vendor communications, interfaces, and problem solving.

Principal Duties & Responsibilities
Coordinates and completes assigned marketing projects for a section or work group within marketing. Provides elementary social media activities to enhance the visibility of the section or work group. Manages and maintains departmental databases and communication files. Handles to completion, customer/client contacts and issues within the assigned scope of responsibility – referring more complex issues to more senior staff. May monitor and report on departmental budgets and defines variances for further action. May provide administrative support to the assigned entity. Performs other related duties as required.

Basic Qualifications & Interests
Possession of a High School diploma or GED. Basic level skill in Microsoft Word (for example: opening a document, cutting, pasting and aligning text, selecting font type and size, changing margins and column width, sorting, inserting bullets, pictures and dates, using find and replace, undo, spell check, track changes, review pane and/or print functions).
Basic level skill in Microsoft Excel (for example: opening a workbook, inserting a row, selecting font style and size, formatting cells as currency, using copy, paste and save functions, aligning text, selecting cells, renaming a worksheet, inserting a column, selecting a chart style, inserting a worksheet, setting margins, selecting page orientation, using spell check and/or printing worksheets).

Preferred Qualifications & Interests
Possession of a Bachelor's degree from an accredited college or university. Previous experience working in marketing, communications, social media, or advertising. Previous experience working in a not-for-profit, NGO, and/or Association environment. Strong project management and basic data analytics skills preferred.

Sample Cover Letters and Resumes

Here are the two sample applicant cover letters.

To Whom It May Concern:

I would like to join ABC Communications as a Marketing Assistant. I believe that my educational background, my internships and other extracurricular experience, and my strong analytical and writing skills will enable me to make a strong contribution to your firm from day one.

As a Communications major at State College, I have immersed myself in the rapidly evolving world of digital media, taking courses including Animation Techniques, Statistics for Media Markets and Survey Research Methodology. I have also been an active writer, with many short and long essays posted at my personal website (www.littleanniesez.com) As a senior I am serving as the editor-in-chief of my school's online journal Music Matters. My writing and verbal communication skills are strong, and I am a fast and detail oriented proofreader.

My analytical and problem solving skills have been tested at internships and in my courses. At JoJo's Bakery, after surveying her customer preferences using a questionnaire I developed, I helped the owner redesign and digitize her promotional materials. Last summer, when I was an intern in the accounting department at Spotify, I honed my project management skills as I helped process invoices and developed a tracking spreadsheet for accounts payable.

As ABC Communications approaches its tenth year in business, it appears poised to grow significantly with the recent announcement of Spotify as a new client. With my strong communications and media skills training and my recent experience inside Spotify, I can bring significant value to the firm as a Marketing Assistant and I look forward to hearing from you.

Thank you for your consideration.

Sincerely,

Annie Smith

To Whom It May Concern::

I am writing to apply for the position of Marketing Assistant with your firm. I am a senior at State College, where I have majored in Philosophy and minored in Psychology and French Literature. During my junior year I studied for one semester in Paris, where I became fascinated by French advertising, especially the way their brands' use of popular music enabled them to reach new audiences. I am determined to start my professional career in public relations because I believe that digital and social media are transforming today's real world applications of the principles of Edward Bernays into ubiquitous and psychologically powerful tools not only for influencing consumer purchases but for molding public opinion and encouraging diverse social behaviors.

Throughout my college career, I have consistently sought out new challenges, and pushed myself to learn new things. For example, I made the Lacrosse team freshman year—even though I had never played before, and I auditioned for and won a role in the senior musical—even though I had never been on stage before. Although my High School did not offer Statistics, I scored well enough on the Statistics AP exam to enroll in Advanced Statistics at State—and I further honed my data analytics skills in both beginner and advanced Psychology courses. I am a self-starter, with strong attention to detail and a powerful work ethic inherited from my father, who started his own company and has always insisted that I earn my own money for school supplies.

I have worked as a camp counselor the past three summers, and have been steadily given more responsibilities at Camp Bellevue. As Head Counselor this past summer, I was responsible for my own bunk of 8 girls as well as for ensuring that the other 7 counselors were able to handle their responsibilities. At Camp B. the counselors and the campers are tasked with a range of camp maintenance projects, from clearing trails to painting sheds. To help keep us on track, I developed an online project check-in system so that we counselors could communicate with each other—and with the camp owner—about our many different maintenance projects in real time. Over the past four winters, I have managed the social media outreach and marketing efforts for Camp Bellevue, and my efforts have resulted in a 15% improvement in camper retention and a 10% increase in new camper enrollment.

The Marketing Assistant position you have advertised in State College's Connect1 system calls for someone with strong project management skills, as well as experience with data analytics and problem solving. I believe that my educational background, my strong verbal and written communications skills, my work experience at Camp Bellevue and my strong interest in the future of advertising well prepare me to hit the ground running for ABC Communications, and I look forward to hearing from you.

Sincerely,

Jill Johnson

Annie Smith

543 Broad St. #1
Anytown, State 12345
123-456-7890
anniesmith1@school.edu

Education   **State College**   Bachelor of Arts, June 2018
College of Liberal Arts and Sciences
Major: Communication | Minor: Animation Studies

Experience **Admissions Office, State College**   **9/16-present**
Assistant
- Draft and edit thank you letters and other correspondence
- Assist with varied administrative projects

Spotify   **May – August 2017**
Intern, Accounts Payable
- Handled all aspects of invoice processing
- Developed tracking spreadsheet adopted for use by management

JoJo Bakery,   **May – August 2016**
Sales and Marketing Assistant
- Sell bakery products in-store, help with catering events
- Created questionnaire and implemented survey of customers
- Helped design and digitize promotion materials

Leadership
and Service **Music Matters**   **Sept 2017- June 2018**
Editor in Chief
- Assign articles to staff writers
- Oversee final edit and proofreading before publishing online
- Worked with local music venues to promote events, obtained discounts for State students

State Mentoring Program   **Fall 2015, 2016, 2017**
Mentor
- Led weekly mentoring sessions for 10-15 first year students

ASPCA   **Fall 2016 - present**
Volunteer
- Help Veterinarians treat incoming animals, work with families as they select pets, assist with administrative tasks in office

Skills

- Photoshop, iMovie, Final Cut Pro, MS Office
- Programming Languages: HTML and CSS
- Social Media and Blogging: Twitter, Facebook, Hootsuite, WordPress, Weebly

Jill Johnson
1234 Center Street
Town, State 54321

321-543-0987   Jjohnson25@school.edu

Education

State College   **June 2018**
B.A. Philosophy Major modified with Psychology and French Literature   **GPA: 3.75/4.00**
   * Study abroad: French Language: Paris, France

College Bound Prep   **June 2014**
* AP exams: 5/5: Microeconomics, Statistics, U.S. History: Calculus BC   **GPA: 4.00/4.00**

Work Experience

Camp Bellevue   **Summers 2015, 2016, 2017**
Head Counselor   Town, ST
- Responsible for ensuring the safety of all camper activities.
- Schedule special events, supervise other counselors.
- Report directly to camp owner; ensure that all maintenance activities are completed on schedule, and manage camp marketing outreach efforts over the winter.
- Act as liaison on behalf of the owner to coordinate visiting special guests such as singers and craftspeople.
- Promoted to Head Counselor after 2 years as Bunk Counselor

Skills and Attributes

Computer Skills: SPSS, Processing 3, Adobe, Photoshop, Premiere, AfterEffects, Audacity, DragonFrame, Microsoft Word, Powerpoint, Excel, Constant Contact, Twitter, Instagram, MailChimp
Languages: Fluent in French
Attributes: Disciplined self-starter, strong team leader, creative team player, extremely well organized, energetic.

Mentoring and Sports Activities

- Academic Tutor and Peer Advisor for first-year students   Spring 2017 – present
- Lacrosse team, member   Fall 2014 – present

Job Interviewing Tips and Strategies

The internet is filled with lists of "top 8 things to do when you interview," or "top 5 things NOT to do"... and most of the advice you will find in these articles is perfectly reasonable.

There is the truly basic advice, such as

- arrive 10–15 minutes early,
- if you have time, use the restroom and do a final check on your appearance,
- dress appropriately,
- get a manicure with no color or a neutral color,
- cover up tattoos and remove piercings, if you can,
- look people in the eye when you are speaking with them and
- project a positive, can-do attitude as you interact with the interviewer.

Then there is even more detailed advice, such as

- exactly what to wear—conservative clothes—usually darker colors,
- how to style your hair: neat and controlled,
- for women, light and natural makeup or perfume, and
- closed toe shoes—yes, really!

The most important thing you can do before an interview is to prepare for it.

Preparation includes:

- Practicing your interview/public speaking skills. You are not memorizing anything but you are practicing speaking fluently on the subject of YOU.
- Plan your answers to likely questions: be ready to explain your academic studies, your recent work background and why you are interested in the position.
- Be your own audience with a mirror, practice with a friend, or use the video playback on your phone.

Golden Tip #17
Never Wear New Clothes (Especially New Shoes) to an Interview.
To be authentic and natural, you need to relax, and new clothes may be uncomfortable or cause you to move awkwardly. On the other hand, you certainly don't want to look scruffy or unkempt! Every season, region and workplace has a dress code—make sure that you only deviate from it in tasteful ways that do not inadvertently cause you to lose status.

- Planning exactly what you will wear, and how you will get to the place so that you are not late.
- Reading. Get up to speed on the company, on the people you will meet with, and on the general industry trends. Prepare some good questions ahead of time as this can help you project confidence.

Golden Tip #18
To Fail to Prepare is to Prepare to Fail.

Don't sabotage yourself by neglecting to prepare for every interview. Focus on the things you can control: **learn** about your interviewer/the company/the industry, **plan** a conservative outfit and make sure it is clean and ready, **prepare** your best answers to likely questions relating to your academic studies, your work background and your interest in the position.

Most people who are looking for a job and going on interviews are not making mistakes about their hair or their clothes. *Instead, they are missing opportunities in the interview to really showcase why they are the right person for the position*.

Why? Because interviews are stressful situations, and we are intimidated into passivity by the combination of wanting to impress the interviewer but at the same time, feeling out of control of the situation.

You can and should develop a personal approach to interviewing that will increase your chances of being selected for the job.

Your goal is to *connect personally with the interviewer* and leave them convinced that you offer the employer something that is essentially intangible—namely, that you are the person among all the candidates who will bring them "what they are looking for" in their new hire.

The key to learning what to do is to realize that "what they are looking for" is not the same thing as "the set of skills that are needed to succeed in the position"—and that although those skills are necessary, they are not sufficient to get you the job.

The foundation of a successful approach to interviews is *confidence*.

Yes, it can be hard to be confident when you are in a stressful interview situation, but you need to work on being comfortable in your own skin.
- Do not give yourself time to dwell on your anxiety.
- Be yourself and just relax into the conversation.
- Do not try to imagine what the next question will be, or offer memorized/rehearsed answers.

- Listen carefully, make and maintain friendly eye contact, and as you answer the questions, try to stay short and on the point and convey that you are a problem solver.
- Don't worry about offering a "right answer"—just speak carefully and tie your answers to the employer's needs as clearly as you can.
- Frame your learning from past experiences positively. Do not say negative things about prior jobs or previous supervisors or colleagues. Tell stories that project your optimism and confidence in your own skills.

Employers want people with passion and enthusiasm.

Passion and enthusiasm are not exactly the same thing. You can show your passion for the field when you talk about yourself, for example in response to an opening interview question of "tell me a little about yourself." Opening with a story about how you discovered your field of interest can give you a chance to speak knowledgeably about the subject, which demonstrates your passion for it.

As you speak, show your sincere enthusiasm and appreciation for the chance to interview for a position where you will be able to realize your passion and work in the area/on the subject that you love.

Interviewers will respond positively to your authentic self.

Authenticity will serve you best when you can offer your friendly and confident self instead of your nervous self—even though of course it is authentic and understandable to be nervous. Just remember that the interviewer is basically trying to see if you will "fit in" to the workplace and if they (the interviewer) would like to work with you. So bring your calmest, friendliest self to the conversation and *remember to relax* so that you will be at your best.

Golden Tip #19
Express Appreciation
Using your Words.

Thank you notes help you build your social vocabulary, and are an important part of building your personal social capital. Stay in touch with people who have met with you and helped you. Sending thank you letters is part of stepping up and taking responsibility for how people will remember you: were you sincere? Did you follow up?

Finally, try to let go of expectations for the interview and go with the flow, remembering that everything is not in your control. If you can ratchet down your anxieties *and* lower your expectations, you should be able to worry less about the outcome of the interview and open yourself up to an easier, more confident conversation. And the more confidence you can project, the more likely that the decision maker will feel that you have that intangible quality that they are looking for!

3 Key Tips for Interview Success

First: Clearly convey that you are a good fit. Tell a story that illustrates how your values align with the firm's, or demonstrate your passion for their mission with an example from your life.

Second: Show that you are listening. Ask a question that follows from what the interviewer has said, even if it's just to ask them to tell you more about something.

Third: Send a thoughtful, professional thank you note within 24 hours. Yes, 24 hours is really the norm, though if you are traveling you can get away with 36–48 hours. You should reference something that was said in the interview in your email.

Writing a Timely and Smart Thank You Note

In most situations, you will address your thank you email formally: Dear Mr. Smith or Dear Ms. Smith, however if the company or the person is obviously more informal, you may address a thank you email as Dear Paul or Dear Suzanne.

Except if you are traveling as noted above, you **must** send this thank you email within 24 hours. I cannot stress this enough. Especially for positions where you will be expected to interact with customers, or develop new business, *management wants to know that you are truly enthusiastic about the position and that you do not procrastinate.* I have even heard that in some places, if candidates don't send their follow up email within the same calendar day they are perceived as slow and may not be selected. The 24 hour rule is an outer time limit, so if you can send a smart follow up email before 8 or 9 pm on the day that you interviewed, you should try do it. Otherwise, the next day, first thing in the morning (8 am–10 am) is fine.

Purpose and Format of a Smart Follow up Email

The purpose of the follow up email is to
- thank the interviewer for the opportunity to meet with them,
- express your sincere enthusiasm for the position and the company, and
- encourage the reader to choose you for the job or at least to advance your candidacy in their process.

The easiest format is a business letter style. Keep in mind that your email may be printed out and/or shared electronically with others in the company.

After the greeting, the first sentence thanks the interviewer, the second sentence says how excited you are about the opportunity, and the third and fourth sentences should offer a smart summary of why you are the candidate they should choose.

Sample Thank You Notes

Here are two sample Marketing Assistant thank you follow up emails:

First Example:

Dear Paul:

Thank you very much for taking the time to speak with me today about the Marketing Assistant position. I came away from our conversation excited and energized by the prospect of joining ABC Communications in this challenging and important role. I really enjoyed hearing about how you won the Spotify business, and I am confident that with my project management experience and passion for superior customer service, I can make a strong contribution to your efforts from day one. I look forward to helping ABC really knock the ball out of the park for this demanding and cutting edge client.

Thank you for your consideration and I look forward to hearing from you.

Sincerely,

Annie Smith

Second Example:

Dear Mr. Jones:

It was a pleasure to meet you today and I came away from our meeting even more convinced that I am destined for a career in public relations! The story you told about how ABC got Spotify as a client really resonated with me as I saw first hand in Paris how critical it was for brands to select the right music to reach their target audiences. I am truly a self starter, and very confident that my analytical skills, my passion for creative approaches to challenges and my strong commitment to a career in public relations well suit me to hit the ground running as your next Marketing Assistant.

Thank you for your consideration and I look forward to hearing from you soon.

Sincerely,

Jill Johnson

What About Your References?

For most positions, you will be asked for professional references. Except for extremely unusual circumstances, you should not offer the names of your family members. If you are interviewing for a position with someone who knows you or your family personally, it may be the case that they will speak with your family, but your professional references need to be impartial. You should always provide three or more non-family references when applying for any position.

You should offer the names of previous supervisors and, if possible, colleagues. Check with your references ahead of time to make sure that they are comfortable speaking about you, and be sure to give them a sense of the new position, why you are interested in it and why you are a good candidate for it.

Sometimes you may be asked to provide references right when you are applying for a job, before you even get to a personal interview. In these cases, the employer will normally state that they will not contact your references without your permission. This gives you time to contact the references after you submit the application.

These days, obviously, employers have a lot of ways to gather information about applicants, and speaking with your references is only part of a larger credential check that they will conduct. **But it is one part of the process that you have control over, so be sure that you are including the people who will speak best for you.** If you have any doubt about that, do not include that person as a reference.

Finally, don't forget to circle back and update the people who care about your professional success. If someone has spoken on your behalf and you got the position, be sure to thank them and let them know how much you appreciate their support. Even if you don't get the position, be sure to let them know and to thank them, since you are likely to want them to speak for you when you apply for another position.

Getting Better All the Time:
More Training, New Credentials

The world is always changing, and to be successful going forward, you will also have to grow and change. I know that it can be exhausting and disconcerting to face the fact that the competitive nature of the work world means that you can never stop *striving*, but that is simply a real world lesson that everyone has to accept.

If this Guide is about anything, it is about the habits of mind and behavior that will help you develop the inner fortitude to face the pressures of the work world. Adopting these habits will give you coping strategies so that this constant pressure to compete doesn't enervate you, but instead, motivates you to improve your skills and up your game. **Chapter Five** is all about the ways you can build your resilience.

One key strategy for improving your competitiveness is to pursue new skills and new credentials. Why and when might you want to consider earning a graduate degree or obtaining additional professional credentials?

There are a few different scenarios to consider.
- You do not start working full time after you graduate from college, and are having a hard time finding a position that earns enough money and offers enough of a challenge.
- You start working full time, but you do not like the job.
- You start working full time, you really like the job and the firm, but you can see that you will more likely be a candidate for promotion at your firm if you earn an advanced degree or take a training program in a specific area.
- You start working full time, you like the job well enough, but you identify the next job you want in a different company and you can see that you will need an advanced degree or at least some additional training.

Golden Tip #20
It's Who You Know
+ What You Know.
We all know the cliché that getting ahead in life is all about who you know. While this Guide emphasizes networking to get ahead in your career, the truth is that building a great career is not only about who you know: *it's also about what you know.* All the networking in the world won't help you if you don't develop some real expertise and the capacity to make a contribution to the work of others.

So you can see that there are a few different situations where it may make sense to consider returning to school for an additional degree, or taking a specialized training program to give you a specific skill set that matches employment opportunities that you would like to explore.

If you are working at a job that you like, and you have the chance to obtain training or enroll in a part time degree program partially or fully reimbursed by the employer, you should strongly consider doing so, since it is *very cost effective for you* to enhance your skill set while you are working.

The challenge is to find the training that suits your aspirations, your available time and your budget. If you do decide to quit work to attend a full time degree granting graduate program, you will need to consider not only the actual out-of-pocket costs of doing so (tuition, housing, books, etc) but also the *opportunity costs* of stepping out of the workforce for a full time student experience.

For **international students** who have decided that they want to stay in the U.S. after they finish college, there is pressure to find a job quickly to stay in compliance with U.S. immigration and visa regulations. But many employers are reluctant to hire international students, for reasons explored in more detail in the **Resource File: Advice for International Students**. For international students, enrolling in a graduate program automatically extends their time in the U.S. and offers them another chance to seek U.S. employment when they finish the second degree.

Every person will make their own calculation of costs and benefits, and remember: there is no single "one size fits all" right way to build a successful career.

Opportunity cost refers to the cost to you if you pursue an opportunity that is different from the one you are pursing now. In other words, if you are working, you have a salary and if you leave work to go back to school full time, you will lose that income stream. The amount of lost income is part of the opportunity cost to you, as is the amount of tuition you will need to pay plus any other new expenses.

Another part of opportunity cost might be *intangible*—for example, you have been living somewhere and establishing a social and professional network there. If you move away to attend school, you may lose touch with some or all of the people in that network. If you have been developing relationships that have begun to generate opportunities for you, but you have not found the right next job, there is a risk that you will lose momentum by stepping back into school.

Opportunity benefit in terms of advanced study seems like it is in some ways easier to picture, but it can be equally intangible. Earning a degree or taking a training class will increase your knowledge about a particular subject area, will give you more credentials on your resume and, hopefully, more skills to offer the market.

If you are a student again, you will have access to student internships, new professors and different career services counselors, a new alumni cohort to network with, and the chance to involve yourself in a wide variety of campus activities, from social events to professional meetings.

Here are some specific factors to consider before spending money on an advanced degree or additional training:

- how much money you are making and what your cost of living is now,
- how much money the training or degree will cost and how you will pay for it,
- how much money you might make after completing the training or degree,
- whether you can combine work and training—remember part time programs that you can complete while still working are very cost effective,

- how stressful it will be to change your living situation, if necessary, and

- how your growing professional network will be affected by your decision.

See the **Resource File: Applying to Graduate School** for specific advice on selecting schools and preparing graduate school applications.

What about Nontraditional Credentials?

As I write this book, there are several changes taking place in the landscape of higher education, including the advent of a wide range of online degree programs, a changing student demographic, and an increasing emphasis on technical/computer skills for recent college graduates regardless of their major. The results of these changes will be far reaching for students and young professionals, not to mention the schools, colleges and universities they attend.

For one thing, as a result of the big data revolution currently underway, many non-traditional credentials are emerging that are dramatically different from traditional diplomas and degrees. Employers are starting to recognize **badges and other non-traditional measures of achievement** as credentials when they review applicant resumes.

Candidates who can offer proficiency with different statistical packages, software applications and/or coding and programming languages will likely have an edge over candidates who lack those skills, where those skills are deemed necessary to the position. Of course, not all entry-level positions will require familiarity with data analytics, coding or social media tools, but an increasing number of firms are looking for these skills.

The obvious dilemma is that the technical skills that are in demand at any given moment may not be the ones in demand in a year or two, and large institutions like universities change their course and degree offerings fairly slowly. Therefore, students and recent graduates who want experience with these new technologies may have to seek out the new organizations and companies that are emerging to offer training in these skills.

It is quite important to be careful when selecting educational programs that are offered outside of the traditional institutions of higher education. Be sure to ask to talk with satisfied graduates and **confirm that employers really have hired people who have completed the program you are considering**.

MOOCs

Over the past few years there has been a lot of media attention to MOOCs and other online courses. MOOC stands for "Massive Open Online Course" and many top universities have begun to offer them directly and through aggregators like Coursera and edX. Many of these courses are offered for free, but if you want to receive credit for the work you do (credit that can be applied to a degree program) or receive a certificate that proves you finished the course, you may need to pay.

MOOCs are a wonderful way to explore a new subject and try your hand at developing new skills with a limited investment of time or money. Each MOOC is different in terms of how it is structured, and the format of online courses is changing rapidly as the technologies evolve to support this new and innovative method of instruction.

Online and Low Residency Degree Programs

Across the U.S.—as well as in the rest of the world—there are an increasing number of schools offering online degree programs. It is no longer considered unusual for top universities to offer full or partially online degree programs. For many people, the combination of convenience and lower costs make for a persuasive argument in favor of earning a degree online. Most of these programs offer degrees that are exactly the same credential as the degrees that could be earned on campus, though there are some degree programs that are only offered online.

Low residency degree programs may offer the best of all worlds. The course work is completed online over a set number of weeks, and then you travel to the campus for one or more short stays. In this hybrid model, you can meet your faculty and the other students in your cohort (those who started the program at the same time as you) in face-to-face lectures and social encounters.

Since one of the most important benefits of doing graduate work is to develop additional professional contacts, programs that support student and faculty social networking will have a lot of attraction for people who have been working for a few years. That could mean immersing yourself full time in a campus environment, taking a part time evening program while you continue to work at your day job, or enrolling in some sort of online degree program. **No matter what program you choose, be sure to take advantage of any social networking that is offered and meet with the career guidance/career services team.**

Every student has to make their own evaluation of costs and benefits when it comes to graduate study—on campus, low residency, or fully online—and the calculation is likely to vary depending on where you are in your career—and your life—when you are making the decision.

What Sort of Training Should Everyone Consider Obtaining?

The explosive spread of digital technology throughout society means that nearly all professional work opportunities in the next few decades will require some familiarity with data analytics. This is because there will be an extraordinary increase in the amount of data and the kinds of data that will be collected as digital sensors are deployed throughout our built environment and in every imaginable industry. All this new data will be combined to create different kinds of timelines of information—all of which will need to be reviewed and analyzed by humans.

Even if you are not planning to be a data analyst, you really do need to know something about what that job function is, and some of its specialized vocabulary.

Try to *gain some experience with data collection and data analysis* through a course in college—psychology courses can be good for this—or try to take an online course when you have the time. You won't regret learning about data analytics and you will enhance your credibility regardless of your major.

These days, it can be hard to avoid stories about how robots are going to take all the jobs away, but I assure you that **humans will always create social and economic value through human-to-human contact**. Experts predict that while many jobs may be taken up by robots and Artificial Intelligence (AI) systems, many new jobs will be continue to be developed in fields and professions we can't even imagine today.

Additionally, while computers and AI will continue to transform the world of work and will eventually capture much of the data collection and even preliminary data analysis assignments, **humans will always be needed to ensure that the real world application of the algorithms' conclusions make sense for the business**.

Robots will never have *Emotional Intelligence*, and as humans build out AI systems to handle the more mundane and easily automated work tasks, it will be human insight, human ingenuity and human empathy that will continue to create — and preserve — value for companies.

Our world will increasingly need people who can explain the results of AI analysis to the managers and leaders in our enterprises. You can ensure that you will be considered for more and more challenging roles if you:

- Enhance your own interpersonal communications skills,
- Strengthen your ability to *learn how to learn* by frequently tackling new subjects, and
- Focus at least a portion of your personal learning on the intersection of data analytics and operations analysis.

Staying Relevant and Competitive

To stay relevant in the world of work, no matter what the field, make sure that you are:

- keeping up by reading widely in your field as well as staying abreast of general business and political news,
- developing your *Emotional Intelligence* through increased self awareness and empathy for others, and enhancing your listening and communication skills,
- learning all you can about AI and data analytics, and
- growing your network so that you have multiple, interlocking circles of people who know and care about you.

Information overload is a real danger. In the old days, a few specialist magazines curated knowledge for us. These days, **you must be your own curator**. *You* need to **find the people who are leading the conversations you care about**, *you* need to follow them on Twitter, and *you* need to read them on Medium and other online and print platforms.

Your relevance and your competitiveness will depend on your ability to increase your understanding and awareness of new ideas, trends, and breakthrough personalities in the areas you care most about.

Join email listserves, Facebook groups or Twitter feeds where there is active participation by thought-leaders.

Chapter Three Take-Aways

1. You can't turn down what hasn't been offered.
2. Spend most of your time networking, not searching the internet for jobs.
3. You can practice crafting multiple cover letters and resume bullets.
4. A job interview situation is a test of fit, not qualifications, so be relaxed and put your best self forward. Smile!
5. Always be learning and consider getting additional credentials and training, especially in Data Analytics.

4 | Finding Your Place in The Real World of Work

This Chapter is about finding your place in the real world of work, which means identifying the types of organizations you might want to work for, figuring out how to overcome obstacles to getting hired, and learning to succeed in diverse workplaces over time.

Identifying Opportunities

The work environment options available to you will vary over time, and will depend on your interests and your real assets.

Think of your assets this way:
- what you have studied/what you are interested in,
- who you know (and who they know!) plus
- how much money you have saved or have access to, and
- when you encounter which sorts of opportunities and challenges.

Additional assets include your health, your "cultural knowledge" which is a function, at least in part, of your upbringing,—and your personal habits of mind and behavior, subjects I explore in detail in **Chapter Five**. As you navigate the world of work and move forward with your career, it's vital to develop a clear sense of your own temperament, your natural aptitudes, your real assets and your enduring interests.

Ideally, you should be seeking *opportunities which will match your personality and your strengths to the challenges of a position within an organization where you can feel validated and supported.* Not every job will be a perfect fit, however you should be able to find positions where you can grow your skills, make a contribution to a larger effort, and support yourself well enough to enjoy a life outside work. Be sure to periodically re-read the strategies for finding opportunities that are detailed in **Chapter Three**.

Golden Tip #21
Cultivate Your Curiosity.

Everyone always says you need to pursue your passion, but what if you aren't sure what your passion is? Don't worry about your passion and instead, cultivate your curiosity! Always be learning and engaging the world on your own terms, and you will make yourself into an interesting and successful person.

On Campus Recruiting: Is It Worth the Time?

One big decision to make when you are still in school is whether to participate in the career service office programs for **on-campus recruiting (OCR).** As you will see later in this Chapter, I recommend trying to work for a large company early in your career if you can, if doing so seems like a reasonable career move given your interests. Therefore, getting hired into a large company right out of school is definitely an attractive option to consider if you are a rising junior or senior and it may well be worth the time and effort to participate in the recruitment program.

Students who have succeeded in obtaining entry level positions with large companies through on campus recruiting programs *uniformly report that doing OCR was like taking an additional course.* They had to devote the same — or even more — time to the recruiting effort as they did to a course. And they had to do it consistently throughout the term even as they were working hard on their other courses. Not everyone who puts the effort into OCR will get a position, however, and one message of this Guide is that there are many different paths forward. So if OCR doesn't work for you — or doesn't interest you — it doesn't mean you won't be able to get a job right out of college.

Staying Relevant: In Person Networking

Staying connected to others **in real life** will help you generate potential opportunities. Be sure to join professional societies and attend their meetings, keep up with your college alumni association (especially helpful if you move to a new city) and participate in local arts and other community groups. You never know where a conversation at the local food co-op will lead.

What Sort of Organizational Role Should You Seek?

No matter what they do or make, most organizations have an *external, public or client facing* team and a set of *internal, functional roles* which support product or service development. When you look at a particular target employer, you should identify and consider different roles within the different departments.

Most enterprises have:

- an executive management team overseeing operations,
- an IT (information technology) services team,
- a Human Resources (HR) function, which in small firms is sometimes combined with other roles,
- a sales or marketing function,
- a quality control or customer satisfaction function,
- an accounting/financial control function, and
- a product or service creation and delivery team.

Figuring out what you want to do for your career includes determining which roles you are most interested in, and most likely to be competitive for, within whichever field or industry you pursue.

Note that many companies (and even non profit organizations) own the real estate associated with their enterprises, so there may be real estate management related functions in the firm, positions which may not be obvious at first glance but which may be interesting and challenging.

In smaller firms, roles may be combined and someone who sells the group's services or products to potential clients may also work on developing those products or services. Different firms use different titles, however it should not be hard to figure out the entry-level positions and the managerial roles at your target organizations—especially now that so much information is posted online.

What people really find hard to figure out is what they truly want to be doing—which is why you should keep an open mind while you network and search for employment—and why going on informational interviews can help you discover roles and careers you never knew existed.

It is very important to take the time to really explore the world of work, since it is the world you will be living in for the rest of your life. Most young people like to do many things and it can be hard to narrow yourself down to just one thing. Reading **Chapter One** and the **Resource File: Key Skill Sets** should have helped you develop a list of possible skills to develop, and you should already have a sense of the industries, issues or topics you are most interested in exploring.

Going forward, you will start to have conversations about specific roles at organizations. When you do go on those interviews, be sure to communicate clearly with the decision makers both why you are qualified for the specific position and how and why the position interests you.

Job interview strategies were reviewed in detail in **Chapter Three**; here I just want to reiterate that when you are talking to a decision-maker, you should express that

- you are able to make a contribution to their efforts from day one, *and*
- you have an interest in further developing the skills and knowledge needed *to be successful in the position*.

It is a delicate balance to strike: on the one hand, you should stress how you are well qualified, right now, to help them meet their objectives, while on the other hand, you should convey that you see yourself learning and growing in knowledge and skills in an area that *interests you and benefits them*. Note, I am *not* saying that you should tell a prospective employer how working in their position will help qualify you for a different position. Rather, I am saying that you should *communicate how you see yourself growing into a strong incumbent in the position under consideration*.

The important thing to keep in mind is that no one expects you to be an expert at a young age. They do expect you to *achieve some immediate goals for the company or organization* while also developing your skills, and expanding your knowledge base. And this is exactly what you should be seeking from your early career employers: opportunities to learn and to grow while contributing to the work of a larger enterprise.

When to Work for Big Institutions, and Why

More than half of the working people in the U.S. are employed by large companies—which are defined as having more than 500 employees. Of course this data includes the many people who work at the retail level for enterprises like McDonald's, Target and Walmart, but it also includes college educated folks working in IT, HR, marketing, facilities operations, management training or other administrative functions such as business-to-business sales.

As a college graduate seeking non-retail employment, **the chances of being hired by a large company are better when you are younger** and recently graduated from school **because these firms have very well developed company cultures and they prefer to hire young and train and promote from within**. They do also hire laterally from each other, so if you start your career in one large corporation, you can advance by moving to a competitor or even transferring your skills to a different industry where the company structures and roles are analogous to your corporate experience and training.

Life in corporate America, which includes working for companies with global scope and operations, is a very specific sort of working experience, and one that many people truly enjoy. Every company is different, but there are some similarities. Most large companies have strong Human Resources (HR) teams so they can:

■ recruit actively both nationally and globally,

■ implement extensive employee training programs, and

■ utilize organizational development strategies to help cultivate the future leadership of the company from within the operational divisions.

Corporate jobs are usually full time positions with substantial company benefits packages, and they usually offer market comparable salaries within an established range. Many large companies offer gyms and wellness programs, company transit—such as buses to train stations—and subsidized cafeterias and other nice-to-have benefits that can substantially improve your working life. Some even offer on-site day care facilities, but unfortunately this is not the norm.

Many large companies are publicly traded, which means that

- the shares (also known as securities) in the company are widely held among the public and traded on the stock exchange,
- the companies are subject to specific government regulations, and
- the companies' management reports to an independent Board of Directors.

Publicly traded companies face close scrutiny of quarterly earnings and other key financial and operations metrics. When the company is doing well, the experience of working there is likely to be pretty positive. When the company is not doing well, there can be a lot of pressure and stress, whether or not your particular job significantly impacts the company's success.

Almost every large company goes through periodic "down sizing" or "right sizing" and re-organization (often called "re-org") in response to challenges in their markets. This regular disruption of the workforce results in lay-offs, *including of employees who have been receiving perfectly fine performance reviews.*

So working for big corporations does have its downsides. However, there are even some positives from this regular "right sizing." For one thing, there are many alumni of the company who have moved on to other companies, and you can usually network into an interview with one of them. Also, downsizing is usually followed by gradual resumption of hiring so while one company is cutting staff, another is probably building up its teams.

As digital technology continues to disrupt the world of established enterprises, it may be that large companies change the way they employ people and/or become less dominant players in the market. For now and in the near future, these full-time plus benefits jobs can be very rewarding both professionally and financially.

Also, and not insignificantly, large companies tend to have well established diversity programs so that **they recruit women and people of color for management roles**. At the same time, they also usually have strong legal protections for their employees so that harassment is not tolerated and promotions are handed out more fairly.

So why should you seek out opportunities with large companies early in your career? In a nutshell, the reasons are as follows:

- **First**, they give young employees substantial training—both on the job and as part of HR benefits packages supporting ongoing skills development;
- **Second**, they usually pay more than comparable jobs in smaller companies;
- **Third**, they offer access to both internal and external advancement pathways—they promote from within and they hire laterally from other large companies; and
- **Fourth**, their regular "re-organizations" generate cohorts of alumni similar to the alumni from colleges and graduate programs—and these alumni can be good networking resources as you go forward in your career and move among different employers.

Finding Jobs with Established Companies and Organizations

When you are in college and thinking about work opportunities after you graduate, you are most likely looking for an existing job with an existing company or organization. By seeking employment from established firms, you are saying to the marketplace that you have a set of skills and interests that match in some way the roles that employers need to fill.

Once you have some idea of the companies that interest you, spend time on their websites, where you can search for open positions, stay abreast of company activities and initiatives, and review the profiles of the company's leadership. In many companies, you can see names and sometimes even profiles for team members throughout the enterprise. You can then search for a particular person on LinkedIn or Google to learn more about them and their network, as a strategy to connect with them for an informational interview.

In addition to the general search advice outlined in **Chapter Three**, if you are still on campus be sure not to neglect these important resources:

- The **Career Services Office**, where most employers post their open positions and conduct information sessions about their companies. Making friends with the career services team is a good idea since they hear about opportunities before they are posted and might give you a "heads up" about a job or an employer visit if they know what you are looking for.

  - It should go without saying that you must learn how to use all your campus' career center resources—especially the automated database of job postings. After all, anything posted in that database is an opportunity to work with an employer that has specifically sought out your school—*they are actually looking for you!* By the way, as an alum you will continue to have access to those listings, though as you age they will become less useful to you.

- **The Alumni Office,** where they want to see you be successful and give back to the school. Learn how to use their resources, and connect with alumni affinity groups focused on particular professions or located in different cities. Try to learn about your school's alumni database and how to access alumni profiles *before* you leave campus. You can use this database to search alumni profiles to identify fellow alumni who work in your target companies and ask them for information interviews. Also, **remember that LinkedIn lets you do searches by school**—so you can find alumni at companies that way too.

Other on campus locations where you might find out about opportunities include,

- professors' offices,
- department bulletin boards, and
- student-run clubs and clinics.

By the way, *department secretaries are an incredible, yet often overlooked resource*, and you should be sure to reach out and make friends with yours!

Overcoming Obstacles

You will face obstacles all along the way to getting hired in your next job, as well as for the jobs after that. The biggest challenge for creating a successful career arc is to find or create the right opportunity at the right time, and this is where it is good to recall Seneca's advice that *Luck is when Preparation Meets Opportunity*. Remember, you only really have control over one thing: yourself, which means focusing your own efforts on being prepared for anything that comes your way.

When you are working hard at a job or at finishing up your degree, it can be time consuming and emotionally overwhelming to look for a new job. So one obstacle is to overcome your own inertia and your own sense of complacency. Remember that nothing is ever fixed in place, and even the best job is going to change over time, perhaps in ways that you won't like. In addition to continuously building your professional network, it makes sense to always be monitoring the market(s) that you care about, watching for opportunities that may come up.

Obstacles to Getting Hired by Organizations

Perhaps the biggest challenge when you apply for an opening at a firm is that there is a lot of competition and the decision maker for the position will likely only see the resumes of a few people who make it through the preliminary screening that the Human Resources (HR) department conducts.

Another big challenge is that many firms will post a position only *after* they have identified a preferred candidate—so the HR screening and the interview process itself may be done very quickly and may be merely perfunctory. Since they have already identified someone as a good fit for the job, they may only be going through the motions to give the process a veneer of respectability/legality. Depending on the nature of the firm and the work they do, they may do this because they have to meet legal process requirements relating to the hiring process. **Of course it is not fair to conduct the process in bad faith, but it is something that all job seekers must be aware of, for several reasons:**

- **If you don't get a call** for a phone interview, it may be because they literally have so many applicants that they don't even get to read your resume and cover letter. To increase your chances of being seen, be sure that you have formatted your resume so that it has the key words and phrases that match their job description—see **Chapter Three** for formatting tips to ensure that your materials will pass through either automated or human HR screening.

- **If you do get an interview** with HR but don't get past HR, it may be because the decision maker has already identified a person they want to hire and your credentials, while impressive enough to get you to a screening interview with HR, are not strong enough for HR to suggest you as a possible alternative to the chosen candidate.

- **If you make it all the way to an interview with the decision maker** but then do not get picked for the position, there can be several possible reasons that do not have anything to do with you or your credentials. For example, the organization may decide not to fill the position because of budgetary concerns; social or political considerations within the organization may favor a different candidate; or as noted previously, the decision maker may have already made up his or her mind before even starting the interview process.

The point of thinking about these possible obstacles is to remind you to stay positive and optimistic! We all think when we don't get picked for something that there must be some problem with us; but the truth is, when you don't get an interview or a job, it often has nothing to do with you. In fact, you should be sure to thank your interviewers no matter what they decide, and reiterate your interest in contributing to their efforts. Be sure to leave on a positive note with them, since you never know when they might have another opportunity to interview you for a different position.

Remember: When one door closes, another opens, and *the right opportunity will materialize for you as long as you maintain your pro-active approach to networking and searching.*

Strategies for Overcoming HR Obstacles

Be Known

Since the vast majority of positions are posted at the *end* of an internal process by which the organization/the decision maker concludes they need to fill a specific role, the best chance you have of being considered is to already be known to the decision maker *before they make the decision to fill the position.*

So, how can you be known to them if you don't already know them? Recall in **Chapter One** I talked about the organizational ecosystem and I said that your goal is to be part of their world. One of the key outcomes of informational interviewing and networking is, hopefully, that you position yourself to be known by decision makers when an opportunity presents itself and they cast around for candidates. Go back and review the networking strategies outlined in that Chapter.

With so many Internet portals available to you (like LinkedIn, topic specific forums and specialized journals, online portals like Medium, etc) there are numerous opportunities to write/publish your ideas. Possible employers are reading these sites and you can become known to them by your original writing or through your comments on others' work.

In 2015/2016, a survey was conducted by The Adler Group in cooperation with LinkedIn and the results confirmed that networking was the most successful job search strategy for all groups of people—those who are actively searching, casually searching or even passively/not searching. The survey also revealed that many employers modify the job requirements to better fit the person they have already decided to hire!

While you are doing all this networking to try to be in the mix before a position is posted, openings will continue to be advertised and you will continue to apply for them. One reason that networking is so valuable is that people who have met you will send you postings for jobs that they think you might be interested in.

Get an Internal Referral

What if a job is posted that you think you are qualified for, but you just don't know anyone (yet) at that organization? How can you increase your chances of being interviewed?

Referred candidates have a real advantage: they are more likely to be hired, and many positions at all levels are filled by referrals. **After you have applied to an open position,** check out the people within the organization as well as the people on its board and look for ways you can network to anyone in the organization. Your goal is to connect personally with someone at the organization, in the hope that doing so will result in HR and/or the decision-maker actually reading your resume!

For example, lets say that you applied for an entry level marketing position, and you ask around and find out that a friend of yours knows someone who works at that company—but in the product development department, not the marketing and sales department.

Reach out and talk to that person anyway—they can tell you about the company culture and give you valuable information about how the hiring process happens—after all, they went through it themselves!

Ask them if they are willing to introduce you to other people at the company, and especially ask them if they know the decision maker in marketing or someone in HR and ask if they would be willing to forward your resume and cover letter to those folks.

An internal referral like this can really make the difference in ensuring that your application is reviewed by at least one human being.

Connect at All Levels

Be sure to review the higher level staff at the organization and explore possible intersections with your network. For example, whether you are applying to a nonprofit or a commercial company, they will have a board of directors. Check out who is on that board. Maybe you know someone (a professor?) who can introduce you to a board member, or to someone who knows a board member...you get the idea. While this sort of sleuthing can be time consuming, it can pay off in several ways.

- You might make a connection that actually gets you an interview for the open position,
- You will expand your network, increase your presence in the ecosystem, and meet interesting people who can give you valuable information about other opportunities that might not yet be public...which is essentially your primary networking goal, and
- Finally, you will be honing your networking and business socializing skills, working on a "muscle group" that is critical to your ultimate career success.

One last possible outcome that can never be discounted: in your networking, you may find someone who decides that they are interested in working with you, and if that person has the power/authority to hire you, you might find yourself with an exciting, unadvertised opportunity. This has happened to countless individuals and reflects the fact that successful people recognize talent when they meet it and will make every effort to bring talented individuals onto their teams.

If you go into all your networking informational interviews with an open mind and a commitment to learning, you will be surprised at what can happen. This doesn't mean asking everyone you meet for a job. In fact, *it's the opposite of that.* You should go into networking meetings simply for the stated purposes of introducing yourself and seeking to learn about the other person. However, you should never approach such a networking meeting casually, or treat the person less than professionally because of the way you got to them (such as through your mom or dad!)

How to Make a Phone Call

These days it seems like no one *talks* on the phone as much as they used to—and some young professionals have literally not had the opportunity to learn how make calls to people they don't know. *The first thing to know is that you can and should use the phone to call people.* In fact, doing so will help separate you from the crowd.

Having said that, it is helpful—whether calling someone you do or don't know—to **set up calls ahead of time**, like this:

- **Send an email** with a subject line like "Talk next week?" for someone you know, or "Referred by John Smith" or "Introduction" for someone you do not already know.
  - **In your email to a friend,** you can suggest some dates and times when a call might be convenient.
  - **In your email to a stranger,** you start with a referral statement or an introduction statement, and then write that you "would appreciate the opportunity to speak with you for a few moments in the next few days (or weeks)" and ask "would it be convenient to set up a call—for example next Tuesday March 22, in the early afternoon? If that is not a good date/time, can you suggest when might be more convenient for you?"
- **When the person emails you** to set up the call, be sure to thank them and confirm the date and time of the call in writing.

- **The day before the call**, send an email with the subject line "confirming our call Tuesday March 22, 1:30pm EST" and in the email a short note reconfirming the call and again thanking them in advance for their time and consideration. You should offer EST or CST or whatever time zone designation makes the most sense for both you and the person.

- **Start the call with** "Hi, this is Jill Jones, is this still a good time for you to speak with me?" If the person hesitates, the two of you can set up an alternative date and time for the call. Be gracious and accommodating, as you never know when you might be the one asking to postpone a call.

- **After the call,** send an email thanking them for their time and following up on anything that might have come from the call. If there was nothing specific that you needed to do (like send the person your resume or a link to your portfolio) then you can just end the email with appreciation and perhaps a promise to keep in touch.

Learning To Succeed

Getting a job and succeeding in a job are only loosely connected. It's similar to the challenge politicians face when they actually win an election and have to switch from the nonstop campaign mode to actually governing. Once you have been hired in a job, the burden is on you to figure out how to succeed. Ideally, the organization and your supervisor will also be focused on supporting your efforts, but you may find, once you get started, that they are not as helpful as you hoped or as they promised they would be.

One key step for you is to define what success will look like both for you personally and what it looks like for the organization. These are definitely not the same thing, however succeeding in meeting the organization's expectations should certainly be an element of your personal success. At the end of the day, your personal definition of success at any given time will reflect where you are in your career and what you hope to gain from taking a particular position.

Golden Tip #22
You Are Joining a Show Already in Progress.
There is a shared history/narrative in the workplace you are joining — be sure to learn your role in the ongoing production so you can demonstrate what a good fit you are for your job. Except for new start-ups, you will join an organization, a team, a hierarchy. Make sure you understand who is officially in charge, who has the real influence and what part you are playing in the show.

Chapter Five offers a detailed discussion of strategies to both make yourself resilient so you can surf the changes at work, and give yourself the tools you need to find personal and professional excellence in your working life.

Benefits of Working With Established Companies and Organizations

Many established companies are well known for their rigorous screening of potential employees and their strong management training programs. If you are selected by one of those companies for an entry-level position, that fact alone will serve you well in the future, not to mention whatever training you receive.

In addition to making sure that you are developing the skills that match the job you are seeking or doing right now, the most successful young people are always seeking to develop the skills for the job they think they might want *next*—after the one they are busy doing or getting right now. As discussed in **Chapter Three and detailed in the Resource File: Applying to Graduate School**, there are many possible additional credentials you may decide you need or want as you progress in your career.

Many employers will support your interest in gaining new skills, and may provide full or partial tuition reimbursement for stand-alone courses, certificates and graduate degrees.

In addition to obtaining financial support for gaining new skills, one of the main benefits of working for established organizations is getting the opportunity to observe the work of those around and above you. What do the people who are just one level senior to you actually do and what are their credentials? How about two levels senior to you or even further up the chain of command?

Successful people turn all work environments into learning environments and in addition to doing the work of their positions, use their time to observe and learn from the people and the interactions around them.

Getting hired is only the first step—not the last—when you join an organization. *It is an even bigger challenge to figure out how to succeed in your role and how to position yourself for your next role—whether within the same or in a different firm.*

In our rapidly changing world, there are no guarantees that any job will last very long, so *you must always be looking out for yourself and for your next opportunity.*

This means that in addition to **doing your best work at all times**, you need to **always be connecting** with new people, so that you are prepared to jump to a new opportunity if your employer announces a lay off or your boss decides to leave and the new boss decides they want to hire an all new team.

Working with and for Start Ups

Although it has always been the case that people with new ideas start their own companies, we now live in a golden age for entrepreneurs. This means that anyone who can start a company probably should try to do so. Some start-ups are created to "disrupt" an existing business and offer something familiar to the marketplace but in a new way. Other start-ups are created to commercialize new technologies, or new products, or new services.

If you are still in school, you are likely to know a few people who are nurturing business ideas. Even if you are not ready to start your own company, you might be interested in joining forces with someone who is. If you are a marketing or management student, think about the people you hang out with—do you know students who are in different programs or do you only have friends within your own major?

Make sure that you have a diverse set of friends and pay attention to people who seem to be full of ideas and energy: those are the people who might start companies. Share your own ideas and your own creative work with your circle of friends and look for ways to support your friends in their efforts. Look for opportunities to build a portfolio of work by volunteering to help on your friend's projects, on projects for school groups, and on projects for community groups.

Many schools have developed *entrepreneurial centers* where students are brainstorming with each other, with faculty and with alumni—and building businesses while they are still on campus.

The culture of start-up companies is very intense, and while the potential financial rewards of being an early hire may be significant, there are also some well-known drawbacks:

- Founders tend to be charismatic, intense people who draw others to them and can expect everyone to work 24/7—the way they do—in support of the mission of the company.
- An all-encompassing work life can be an exciting and emotionally rewarding experience—or it can lead to frustration and burn out.
- Start-ups are notorious for failing. You may find that after working non-stop for a year or two the business closes down and you are left looking for your next gig despite the fact that you were doing excellent work.

Many young people are drawn to the start-up world for the same reasons that people love to be part of theater productions: they get pleasure from the work and develop intense relationships with co-workers who become like family after many days and weeks of working closely together day and night. If you find that you are in a position to join a start-up, be sure to carefully consider both the opportunity *and* the opportunity costs.

Finally, remember that everyone you know now will be moving around the marketplace over the next few years. You never know where a future opportunity might come from. By staying loosely connected to lots of people through social media, you can be recommended by a friend when they hear of an opening or need some help on a project.

Nonprofit Organizations

Nonprofit organizations in the United States are incredibly diverse. The designation as nonprofit means that:

- the organization has been created with the express understanding that any surplus revenue that is generated by its activities will be reinvested in the organization and not distributed to its owners, directors or other people, and

- at least in the U.S., the organization will be exempt from paying taxes on its income and assets, and people will be able to take tax deductions for any donations they make to it.

In general, nonprofit organizations tend to be focused on addressing social problems, however the category is actually very diverse. There are small and large organizations, including philanthropic, religious and educational institutions. There are small, local charities run mostly by volunteers, and there are large foundations with million dollar endowments. Some nonprofits are very large enterprises, and can be similar to major corporations in their hierarchical management structures.

Salaries at nonprofit organizations tend to be lower than at commercial enterprises, though the actual work of comparable entry-level jobs may be similar. To justify lower salaries, incumbents point to the psychic rewards of working with an organization that is trying to solve social problems. Finally, nonprofit organizations often have generous benefit policies and friendly working environments.

Building a career in the nonprofit world requires all the same outreach and networking as you would use in the commercial world. In fact, sometimes the competition for nonprofit jobs is *more* intense than for business positions. This may be because of the perceived status associated with working for an admirable organization committed to solving social, environmental or economic problems.

Social Entrepreneurs

Social entrepreneurs are people who bring innovative thinking to social, cultural and environmental challenges. They often use the extraordinary potential of digital technologies to address social problems, and they are creating new kinds of companies to support their efforts. A lot of this creative thinking is happening in engineering programs, but budding social entrepreneurs can be found in programs as diverse as the arts, mathematics or social work.

Ashoka is a well-established organization that helps identify and support social entrepreneurs around the world. Ashoka helps innovative "change-makers" focus on systems-level solutions. You can learn more about social entrepreneurs at www.ashoka.org and at www.Changemakers.com.

You are Always Working for Yourself

For most students and recent graduates, going out on your own as your own boss is not an immediate goal. For one thing, most young people don't have an area of expertise that they can reliably sell to others—though an obvious exception is tech-based skills like the coding needed to build web sites, where many young people are expert enough to gain clients and projects.

Aside from a perceived lack of expertise, the main reason most young people do not start their careers as independent consultants is that their networks are not large enough to generate regular assignments from a wide range of clients.

But…if you find yourself struggling to find a full time job, you may find that working short "gigs" for others is a good way to establish yourself as a young professional in your community. You may find gigs doing tech based projects or writing or social media outreach or other professional work.

In fact, even when you do have a full time job, it's a good idea to go to work everyday with the thought in mind that **you are always working for yourself.** Despite the hype and excitement that surrounds joining teams within companies and organizations, in practical terms it makes sense to stay focused on the fact that, ultimately, even when we are working for social good, we work for our own financial benefit and personal satisfaction.

We are in the habit of saying we work "for" a company, since when we take a job the employer pays us for our time and our efforts. However, it's important to recognize early in our working lives that while meeting our employer's expectations is necessary to succeed in a particular position, what's truly needed to succeed in life is to meet—and even exceed—our own *personal* expectations.

Most of the time, your personal and professional expectations are aligned, which is great. But you will have many jobs over the course of your career, and it is likely that you will have some less than perfect job experiences…so you also need to remember that *your worth is not determined by your job* and you must build and enjoy a life outside of the workplace.

See **Chapter Five** for notes on how to develop the habits of mind and behavior that will sustain you when you experience career setbacks, and see **Chapter Six** for notes on developing a satisfying integration of work and life.

Golden Tip #23
Think of It as
"Me, Incorporated."
Successful careers are deliberate creations. You must take a business—like approach to your career, anticipate the obvious challenges, make decisions rationally, and take pro-active steps to ensure your success, happiness and financial well-being. Think of it as building a company that is called "Me, Inc." If not you, then who?

Succeeding in Multicultural and Diverse Work Places

Working in the U.S. means working with Americans as well as with the many people who come to work in U.S. companies from all around the world. Americans are not a homogeneous people, and a significant number of Americans are first or second generation immigrants representing every country in the world.

Over the past fifty years, the American corporate business world has implemented some very progressive and supportive employee support policies. However, corporate culture — the norms and expectations of people who work in big corporations — is not the same as American culture. While there will be some similarities, it would be a mistake to assume too much commonality among employment experiences in different sized firms throughout the fifty states. Working conditions and business practices are not uniform and will likely vary substantially from one location to another and between one firm and another.

In both corporate jobs as well as in smaller firms, it is important to find ways to co-exist with — and even embrace — the dominant cultural norms, without losing your sense of personal and cultural identity. It's very important to have a sense of when and how to *flex your style* so you can succeed in the work environment — but of course you should never allow yourself to be bullied or harassed.

While the dominant cultural norms are always evolving, there are some common dimensions to most U.S. workplaces that are important to be aware of as you go forward in your career.

- English is the language of business in the US.
- White heterosexual men still hold the majority of top positions, though there has been significant progress in diversifying company management.
- Fitting in to the office culture is critically important, and someone is considered a good fit for the company/their job if they can get along with the bosses and co-workers.

- Especially in large corporations, you are likely to have coworkers and supervisors of varied race, gender, sexual orientation or ethnicity, and it is important to recognize and overcome your own biases toward others.

- Incompetence is not a barrier to promotion (this is true in every country!)

If you have a problem with a supervisor or a co-worker, you should be cautious and use discretion if you decide to approach HR. If you cannot speak to your own manager because they *are* the problem, or if your manager doesn't solve your problem, HR *may* be able to help, especially in large firms.

It's important to remember that HR personnel represent the company and are always seeking information about employee performance, so, for example, if you are being harassed, they will want to know about it— both so that they can try to help you individually, and so that they can help protect the company from a rogue employee.

Expressing Yourself at Work

While finding opportunities to fully express yourself in life is certainly important for your overall mental health, it is usually not appropriate to pursue self-expression on the job. Indeed, to succeed professionally it is often necessary to suppress some dimensions of your personality at work.

Everyone has to find the right *persona* to bring to work, and it is not going to be the same *persona* that you bring to a party. That doesn't make your work self a false *persona*—it just means that you are taking the time to read the environment and finding your own way to fit in and succeed. You are not giving up your identity when you go to work, but you are *flexing your style* so that you will succeed in the work environment.

"Code switching" is an expression describing the activity of using one vernacular and way of communicating when you are with one group—and then switching to another mode when you are with a different group. It can include suppressing some dimensions of your personality to succeed in the dominant culture, and it can be exhausting. Be aware of this pressure (if you feel it) and be sure to find peer support groups so you can find places to safely vent any frustrations you may feel.

Social media activity can be a minefield when it comes to self-expression.

- It is very easy to express yourself with "likes" and by forwarding things you approve of, find humorous, or find appalling.
- It can be very challenging to maintain boundaries between work and personal life when you are Facebook friends with co-workers.

When you do send co-workers these expressions of your opinion, you are not asking them for their permission, and you may be inadvertently creating awkward or even unpleasant associations for them. Be very cautious about sharing funny pictures, news articles, etc. with co-workers.

Remember that everything you do on a work computer, laptop or mobile device is trackable by your employer and, if not work-related, could be considered inappropriate personal use.

Finally, as a reminder, there are a few topics that are not considered appropriate for small talk at work. Traditionally, these forbidden topics are sex, politics and religion. But you do want to make small talk with your co-workers, because it is a good way to demonstrate fitting in. Whether in person or on social media, you can never go wrong with sports, the weather, or recent or favorite films or TV shows.

Chapter Four Take-Aways

1. Know yourself: have a clear sense of your true assets and interests
2. Stay optimistic and pro active and remember that when one door closes, another opens.
3. NETWORK * NETWORK * NETWORK
4. Remember that you work for yourself even as you work with others
5. Use discretion in all communications and try to maintain boundaries between work and personal life.

5 | Enhancing Your Personal Resilience

When life hands you lemons, you make lemonade, right? Sometimes, a lay-off is a welcome nudge…if you are prepared financially and you are able to quickly get another position. But sometimes getting laid off feels like a real career setback, and getting fired can be an even tougher blow to your finances, not to mention your self-esteem.

Many people are traumatized by bad employment experiences, and even the most successful young professionals can go off course. How will you survive and even thrive as you surf your way through life's challenges? This chapter explores how successful people prepare themselves to compete and win even as the world offers its inevitable setbacks and disappointments.

Hiking without a Map

Starting your career is like beginning a journey with no clear picture of the destination in mind and without a reliable map in hand. You are compelled to start walking, but you are not sure where you are going nor what you will encounter along the way. Although there may be a progression of job titles that you identify as a career path you wish to follow, *your career is not a series of job titles*: it is more like a lifetime hike through unknown territory!

Some people find the entire career discussion quite overwhelming, and they experience a lot of anxiety as they try to figure out what to focus on as they contemplate the end of their academic programs. Mental health counselors on campus or in your community can help you work through your emotions and help with your planning. If anxiety is preventing you from even thinking about career planning, be sure to talk with someone who can help you.

After you graduate, it can be unsettling to start your career with one expectation in mind, but find after one or a few years that you are not happy with the direction it is taking. Maybe you are getting bored or just don't like what you are doing, and you can't see how this job will get you to something better. It can feel like you are lost, and this lost feeling can get worse if you seem to be the only person in your world who doesn't already have their career all planned out.

We all know a few people who seem to be sure of themselves from an early age, with a clear idea both of their chosen profession and of the path to achieve their objective. The good news is that if you don't have your life's work clearly envisioned and your entire career mapped out **you are not alone**. Even for those who have it all planned out, life has a way of surprising us and upsetting even the best laid plans. And besides that, experts say that many of the jobs people will have in ten or twenty years don't even exist today.

So the primary challenge in your first few jobs after college or graduate school is simply to do your best work and try not to worry too much about not knowing exactly what you want to do with your entire life. Even if you have taken a job that didn't match exactly what you had in mind for yourself, as long as you are developing new skills and demonstrating your capacity for excellence to your supervisors and colleagues, you will gain valuable professional and personal experience.

You will succeed in the long run by leveraging all your experiences, including the experience of working at a job you may not love.

The Real Power of Positive Thinking: Framing and Re-Framing your Experiences

You must take whatever steps are necessary so that you stay physically and mentally healthy and keep a positive attitude about yourself and your career. It is critically important that you be honest with yourself and hold yourself accountable for all your behavior, however, at the same time, *you should also be compassionate with yourself*. This doesn't mean letting yourself slide when it comes to fulfilling responsibilities to yourself and others, but it does mean to take it easy on yourself when bad things happen. **Good people can make mistakes, and bad things can happen to good people without any warning**.

By mentally preparing yourself, you can help minimize your risk of being traumatized when life's inevitable disappointments arrive. Preparation includes always learning new skills that can lead to new opportunities, and, perhaps even more crucially, preparing yourself mentally, psychologically and emotionally for the challenge of re-framing your personal narrative when things don't go as planned.

We constantly tell ourselves stories about our lives—whether we are day-dreaming, brainstorming, or "Blue Skying"—as we identify our goals and objectives and make our plans and dreams. Short term, long term, Plan A, Plan B… your "self talk" is very important to your mental well-being, and **you need to take control of what you tell yourself and what you tell others about your career**.

Be very mindful about how you frame past employment experiences and *consciously tell a progressive story*—no matter how bad an experience was, there is some lesson you can draw from it, and some positive way you can describe it. No one likes to work with a person who speaks poorly of herself or of her past work experiences. If you badmouth past colleagues or bosses to new or potential colleagues, they will consciously or unconsciously think "is this how she will speak about *me* in the future?" and this will cause them to be wary of you.

So, no matter how bad your old boss was, or how crazy the work situation, be cautious in how you describe it to others. Don't dwell on past negatives; pivot conversations to future oriented questions and positive observations.

As you frame your experiences for yourself and others, keep reminding yourself:

- You are a good, hardworking person,
- You have succeeded in the past (rewind your greatest hits in your head), and
- With a good night sleep, you can face any challenge with grace.

This Guide supports the idea that successful careers are deliberate creations within the real world life context of random occurrences of incalculable odds. While you must take responsibility for what you are doing, you cannot control what the world will do with you—or to you. **The only thing you can control is how you react to the world: You can control yourself.**

Successful people maintain control over their reactions to both good and bad news, and they don't let the inevitable setbacks of life stop them. It can be hard to get up the next day and go back to work after you have had a bad day or even a bad review—but you can find the strength inside yourself…and you must do it!

Developing Aristotle's "habit of excellence" will not protect you from bad bosses and bad experiences, but it will help you *maintain your self-respect* and give you the energy and discipline to keep going…to prevail on another day—or in another job.

Staying Competitive, Agile, and Relevant

The Internet has changed the world in many ways. The speed of change, both in society and in the market, is one the hallmarks of the 21st century. Companies that were hot a few years ago are already history, and new innovators are transforming our lives in big and small ways everyday.

Golden Tip #24
Life is Random,
Your Response is Not.

Life may be a series of random occurrences of incalculable odds, but how you marshal your intelligence and your energy to respond to life's challenges is totally up to you.

110

In terms of job hunting and career progression, one of the most significant changes brought by the Internet is the easy availability of an incredible amount of information about companies and individuals.

You already know that you need to

- **continually educate yourself** about the ecosystem of organizations and people in the fields that interest you, and
- **read the biographies** of people in positions that you are interested in to figure out possible alternative career pathways, and potentially useful degrees and certifications, and
- **continually do outreach** and grow your network, both in person and online, so that you are aware of the trends, the issues and the latest news relating to the people, the companies and the issues that you care about.

These ongoing activities are "must do items"—**but why?**

The answer is that if a person *could* easily find things out, but fails to do so, it will reflect badly on them…and the odds are very good that there is a competitor out there who *will* be current with the latest news about companies and gossip about people.

Therefore,

- You *must* seek out all the information available to you to ensure that you stay competitive and employable throughout your career, and
- You *must* prepare yourself mentally and emotionally for a lifetime of job hunting by *developing the habits of mind and behavior* that will keep you competitive, agile and relevant.

In sum, *even when things are going well*, you still need to be reading, learning, networking and building the social ties that will help you be aware of and compete for opportunities. And you need to develop daily habits that will strengthen you and prepare you for both success and inevitable setbacks.

Building Resilience:
9 Key Habits of Mind and Body

What is resilience? A good working definition is *flexibility and strength in the face of obstacles and challenges.* Over the course of your career, you will need to be personally resilient so that you can continue to earn a living and live a life that is full and satisfying. To consciously build personal career resilience and enhance your own inner psychological strength, develop these *9 key habits of mind and body.*

1. Compete at Peak Physical and Mental Health

You will have a difficult time thriving and competing if you often find yourself under the weather or so sick that you miss work. So staying healthy enough to show up to work is an obvious priority, but *you need to do more than stay out of the doctor's office to thrive and succeed in today's competitive marketplace.*

Your goal is to operate at your own level of high/peak performance every day.

What this means for each person is a little different, so you need to be brutally honest with yourself. Remember, you are a smart person who will make your living *by your wits*—that is, by using your brain power as effectively and efficiently as you can. Only you know what your head feels like when you wake up in the morning, so no one else can tell you when you need to take a break and recharge your batteries.

■ **You need a schedule**. If you are holding down a full time job (maybe for the first time?) you are going to have to **build—and stick to—a schedule** for yourself that includes sleep, exercise, friends and alone downtime so that you can effectively recharge and show up at work with the mental energy and emotional strength you need to excel at your work and shine in your personal interactions.

- **You need to nurture yourself**. You can never succeed in the long run if you burn yourself out in the short run. It is easy to fall into over-working traps, and for many people, more hours working translates directly into cash in their pockets, so it is easy to understand why they take on more shifts and add part time gigs to their weeks and weekends. However, recognizing that you have to support yourself financially does not mean abdicating responsibility for taking care of yourself physically, emotionally and psychically.
- **You need to develop habitual self-care strategies** that will help you cope with the day-to-day grind of the challenging work environments where you hope to succeed and prosper.

It is critical to remember that, except for your family, no one really cares that much whether you succeed or not...so *you need to care about and for yourself with a fierce energy and passion that will enable you to overcome all the haters, naysayers and sheer indifference you will encounter in the world.*

2. Develop and Use Self Care Strategies

What are examples of *self-care strategies* that can build your personal resilience? There are as many different strategies as there are people, so you will need to figure out for yourself what works best for your person-ality, as well as any constraints on your energy, time and money.

The important thing is to **make self-nurturing a regular routine**. In this way, when the hard times come, you will have built up a practice of self-care that will sustain you as you work through the inevitable chal-lenges of a difficult supervisor or colleague, unexpected unemployment, or health or relationship struggles.

The wide range of possible self-care practices includes everything from daily running to weekly meetings with a therapist or a career coach. You should try to get regular exercise, see friends outside of work, try to relax *without alcohol* as often as possible, and *most importantly, get enough sleep.*

Sleep: Almost nothing you can do for yourself is as important as getting enough regular sleep—7, 8 or even 10 hours every night. And by the way, the sleep clock is a 24 hour master: you cannot make up on the weekend what you miss during the week, and you cannot make up during the week what you miss on the weekend.

■ *Set a regular bedtime and stick to it as much as you can.*

Caffeine: Caffeine is a stimulant, a drug that we ingest day after day practically without realizing it. Since so much of your career will be spent networking over coffee, I am hardly going to tell you to stop drinking it. But it is important to keep in mind that for most people, too much caffeine in a day, or over a few days, will negatively impact their ability to fall asleep. As a result, they may sleep fewer hours and then find themselves needing more caffeine in the morning so that they can be alert. Drink decaffeinated beverages whenever you can, but especially in the afternoon and evening.

■ *Avoid creating a vicious cycle for yourself that has you sleeping poorly and over-doing the caffeine just to keep up with your daily routine.*

Alcohol and Drugs: Most college students drink socially and many use marijuana or other drugs, such as prescription stimulants, on a regular basis. One of the hallmarks of growing out of the student life is cutting back on the recreational use of alcohol and drugs, at least during the work week. Keep in mind the following points:

■ Many employers will use drug tests to screen out applicants, and while alcohol use is not generally an issue, marijuana smoking can prevent you from getting a job offer or cause you to be dismissed.

■ Even in states where there is legal medical use of marijuana, private employers can set their own rules and may choose not to hire people who test positive for marijuana, regardless of medical necessity.

■ Claiming marijuana as a medical necessity means identifying yourself to the state and potentially to the federal government as a marijuana user.

While I recognize that medical necessity is a real thing, the fact is that the legal status of marijuana is currently in flux, and therefore the future legal status of marijuana is unknown. It appears that more and more states are legalizing its use both for medicinal and recreational purposes, however we cannot predict whether this trend will continue, or be reversed, nor whether the federal government will follow the lead of the states and legalize its use.

The future use of any digitized information regarding medical marijuana is hard to predict, however

- We do know that insurance companies already use digital medical records to screen potential customers,
- Being on an official medical marijuana list would likely prevent future employment by a state or federal government agency,
- Being on a medical marijuana list may disqualify you from working in such professions as medicine or engineering, or in defense related industries—including consulting—which may require government security clearances, and
- If you have obtained a medical marijuana card and then apply to attend law school/practice law in the United States, there are various state specific required "character and fitness" disclosures, which may complicate your admission to the Bar.

Finally, while marijuana is not believed to be harmful to your health, it is commonly associated with lethargy and lack of ambition.

Getting on an official list of marijuana users is a risk to your future career prospects. It is a risk that some people will choose to take, but I strongly urge you to consider all possible alternatives before you choose to do so.

Exercise: Most of us work at computers and we are either sitting or standing when we do it. Too much sitting is the cause of a lot of back problems, over time it can be the cause of weight gain, and it is just generally not good for your health to sit at a computer all day long, five days a week. Try walking briskly each day for at least 30 minutes, work out at a gym on a regular basis, swim laps, play basketball, go to kick boxing or aerobic workout classes, or develop a yoga practice.

■ *It doesn't matter what exercise you do, just do it regularly.*

Focused Downtime Activity: Everyone needs to have some down time that is not work but that engages you fully in a way that takes you away from your daily world. You could learn to knit, cook, draw or paint pictures, throw pots or develop some other crafty skill (glass blowing anyone?) Most sports, arts and exercise regimes will give you a break from your work thoughts, too, which is a key element of strategies for staying creative. The ideas are as endless as your imagination.

■ *It doesn't matter what you do to unwind, just do it regularly.*

Mindfulness: Learn to incorporate mindfulness in your life. Being mindful means finding ways to slow yourself down as you encounter the world, and it can include learning to meditate, practicing gratitude and developing the habit of taking deep breaths to calm down when you are feeling stressed.

■ *There are many books and resources on mindfulness, which can help you develop coping skills for emotionally difficult situations.*

Cooking: Learning to cook is a great downtime activity, and an easy way to bring better, healthier food into your life. It is fun to learn and it is satisfying to do alone or with friends. You do have to invest in some household staples like oils and spices, but they are called staples because they have long shelf lives. When you are cooking, the senses are engaged in ways that really benefit your peace of mind, and you can enjoy eating the results of your efforts. So go online and look up the recipe for something you like to eat and give it a try. Ask for a cookbook for your next birthday and learn to make a few of your favorite dishes.

We live in a world in which fast, cheap but not so healthy food is all around us, and it can be very easy to fall into bad food habits. Whether living alone or with others, it can seem very difficult to cook meals during the week, and on the weekends we like to go out and have fun, which usually includes eating in restaurants.

Further, when we are stressed we often seek out "comfort foods" which, depending on your upbringing, might include donuts, cookies, french fries or other satisfying and easy to get treats, which are fattening and don't offer us the nutrition we need.

- *Cooking can help you eat like the physical and mental competitor you want to be!*

3. Integrate Technology Best Practices

As computers and mobile phones have become ubiquitous in our world, it has become more important than ever that we develop good habits to control our interactions with these devices.

For many people, the mobile phone is their constant companion. It is the first thing they see in the morning and it is the last thing they look at as they go to sleep. A significant number of people do not turn their phones off at night, and will admit that they answer or at least look at text messages and even emails if the phone alerts them in the middle of the night. Of course even if you don't look (and who can resist?) your sleep will have been disturbed, contributing to the sleep deficits that so many people experience.

Each of us has to develop their own approach to handling mobile phones, and our strategies can and will change as our circumstances evolve. You need to be aware of the negative effects of continually check-ing the phone for Facebook updates, new work emails, or text messages from friends.

These **negative effects can include**:

- **Increased levels of stress**—and specifically, stress to your fingers, to your eyes and to your neck as you look down.
- **Dry and painful eyes**—even if you don't wear glasses or contact lenses, if you use a smartphone or work on a computer you are constantly exposing your eyes to blue light, and most likely not blinking enough.
- **Insomnia, anxiety and depression.**
- **Difficulty relating to other people.**
- **Giving up on figuring things out for yourself** because you are looking to the computer or cell phone for all the answers, and
- **Failing to fully engage when you socialize** with others because many people cannot ignore their cell phones even when they are with their friends.

Schedule and Take Technology Breaks

It should go without saying that it has always been the case that the more authority and responsibility you have at work, the more you need to be connected to the office even when you are officially on vacation. In our digitally interconnected world—where emails and text messages create unsynchronized yet detailed communication with colleagues—your boss may well email you when you are out of town, or in the middle of the night.

The pressure to be constantly checking your phone to see if you have new email is a very real stressor. So a key challenge these days is to find ways to balance the insatiable demands of work with our needs for physical, psychological and emotional recharge. One way to create the balance that we all need is to ensure that you carve out "no phone/no computer" times—every day, every week—and use that psychic space and that disconnection, to reconnect with the people and the activities that can offer you a respite from work and career worries.

Schedule regular technology breaks each day and each week. That can mean a phone free dinner each week, an entire day computer and phone free, or chunks of time throughout the day where you do not check email. Whatever you choose to do, make it a habit and closely safeguard the time you can steal from the digital world!

When you are working on a computer, it is a good idea to look away from the screen every 20 minutes. Some people set their phone alarm for 20 minute segments, and then focus on something in the distance. Maybe stand up and stretch, or even take a walk around the office for a few minutes.

Practice Good Technology Hygiene

In addition to being mindful about the impact of technology on your health, it is very important to develop good technology practices in terms of which devices you use for which purposes.

- **Don't ever — ever — use the work computer to do anything personal. *Period.***
- Don't use a work computer or employer-owned laptop to send personal email, surf and/or shop, or post comments on any site, ever. Not on a news site, not on Reddit, not on Facebook.
- If you are issued a work laptop or mobile device, don't ever — ever — use it to do personal email, surf and/or shop, or post comments on any site, ever.
- No personal work or fun on employer-owned devices. Period.

Why am I saying the same thing multiple times? Because if an employer is unhappy with you for any reason, and you have used their technology for an unauthorized purpose, they can fire you with no questions asked. And yes, they can do that. And yes, they are monitoring the computer use of employees, and if they decide to look, they can find out every site you visited, and every comment you made.

Many employers periodically seek to reduce their staffing levels, and they may very well look into technology use as part of their internal assessment of whom to keep and whom to let go. **Don't inadvertently sabotage yourself** by shopping on Amazon or checking Facebook on your work computer. Also, keep in mind, clearing your search history from an employer's laptop or desktop computer doesn't clear it from the employer's system.

Go back and review the advice about cleaning up your digital footprint from **Chapter Two**, and make sure that you are maintaining best digital practices at work.

4. Use Discretion To Compete in the Real World

The truth is, the world is much more competitive and cutthroat than anyone ever admits. People above you are competing with each other to go higher and make more money, so they may exploit you for their own benefit. People at your own level or below you are competing *against you*, regardless of how many team-building and trust building exercises you participate in.

There are usually limited opportunities for promotion in a particular office, though in big companies there can be a lot of lateral movement from office to office. You have to take care of yourself so that you can be agile, relevant and strong in the face of circumstances which are usually beyond your control, and may be overtly hostile or at least indifferent to your success. Office politics can be unpredictable and vicious, so you need to keep yourself mentally, physically and emotionally prepared.

Does this mean that you cannot be friends with people at work? Definitely not—but it does mean that you need to be judicious *even with your friends* about what you share of a personal nature. Remember: no one is perfect and a friend could make a mistake and share your private information with someone else at work—even if you told your friend it was a secret.

Golden Tip #25
You Are on Their Team but They Are NOT on Your Team.
Remember: It's Me Inc., no matter what your paycheck says. While the employer paying you rightfully expects your professional loyalty, this does not mean that you should trust them with any of your *personal* dreams, plans or ideas. Never share your thoughts about a potential job change, a move out of town or overseas, or plans for going back to school—until you are literally ready to resign.

What are the personal things you should not share? Well, the most important subjects to be careful about when you are in your first few positions are:

- looking for a new job
- going to graduate school
- significant unhappiness in your personal life or your childhood
- excessive drug or alcohol use

Never tell anyone at work that you are looking for a new job or going back to school unless you are resigning from your job that day.

If the topic of additional training comes up in a work setting or with work friends after hours, you can share that you are always seeking out opportunities to learn, but do not share that you are talking to anyone about a particular position or have applied to graduate school and are awaiting the admissions and financial aid decisions. This is especially true if you are talking with HR or company managers about possible opportunities or promotions within the same organization.

The reason you are not sharing this news… is that you do not have the news to share yet. Once you have made a decision about leaving your current job, you can talk about it—but not before you have accepted the offer or sent your deposit to the school.

Don't use your co-workers as a support group for your personal problems, and don't gossip about your co-workers with your outside friends either.

You never know who will connect with whom. Even only slightly derogatory comments you may have made casually can come back to bite you in the future. The world is actually very small—and it is getting smaller everyday as social media knits everyone closer and closer together.

You can never be too careful when it comes to sharing details about your personal life at work. No one needs to know very much about your roommate problems, your family issues or your love life. Keep your comments light, keep them short, and keep your most intimate concerns to yourself. When in doubt about what to share in response to a personal question, share very little and pivot to asking that person a more general question.

It really is best to pick a few neutral topics to share, like local sports teams and local weather, funny television shows, crazy things your friend's cat did. Don't gossip about others at work, and try to never ever discuss politics, religion or sex.

Of course, the working world is not entirely cut throat and mean spirited, and finding allies at work can help you succeed in your job and can help make work fun, which is always a good outcome. In fact, over the long run, remaining socially friendly with allies from prior positions is very strategic. Maintaining loose yet amicable ties with many people can help generate new opportunities as you move forward in your career.

5. Circulate and Be Known to Others in the Office

Many jobs these days require less and less "face time" in the office, and formal, scheduled interactions with colleagues and superiors may be minimal. It is not in your interest to be unknown to the powers-that-be in your workplace. In fact, especially if you have an entry-level position that doesn't require very much interaction with management, you need to make sure that you are on their radar as a productive and positive energy team member. You can do this by participating in whatever open group activities there are—from birthday parties to team sports to fund raising efforts.

Also, be sure to be friendly and respectful to everyone you meet—from the mailroom team to the receptionists and even the office cleaners if you meet them after hours. *Being known as a nice person never hurt anyone* and, in fact, can turn out to be a secret weapon in office politics, because you never know when your name might come up and someone may offer an opinion about you. The original Golden Rule should always be your guide: treat other people as you would like to be treated yourself, and avoid gossip!

6. Always Be Learning

Throughout your career, no matter what position you have, you must keep developing new skills so that you are prepared for any career enhancing opportunities that come your way. This **on-going personal skills development program** is the backbone of a successful effort to build up career capital.

What sort of skills should you develop? Look at the job requirements for the positions that you hope to move into next. You should also follow up on subjects that may have come up in your informational interviews.

Here are some categories to consider as you think about how to structure your continuing education:

- New computer skills, including data analytics and even coding
- Project management certifications
- Common office software, including programs like MailChimp, or InDesign
- Any specific certifications that are related to your discipline
- New languages—computer and human

Learn Across Multiple Fields

Elon Musk developed four major multibillion dollar companies by his early 40s in four diverse fields: software, energy, transportation, and aerospace. Aside from the fact of his extraordinary personal productivity, one key to understanding his breakthrough approach to achievement is to recognize that he did not follow traditional guidelines for developing expertise. He did not limit his learning to one field of study, but rather throughout his life, Musk has read widely and deeply in multiple domains.

What is the impact of reading widely and deeply across multiple disciples? It means that, compared to other experts in a particular field, Musk was able to bring insights from his cross trained mind to bear on new challenges. This is called "learning transfer" and it enabled Musk to take what he learned in one context and apply it to another.

You, too, can cross train yourself, and read widely and deeply in more than one field. By giving yourself this life long habit of curious investigation of more than one subject at a time, you will give yourself an edge in your own main discipline when compared to others in your field. You will be able to apply insights learned from diverse books or training courses, which can foster your own breakthrough creativity and help you stand out from other competitors.

We know that professionals in the 21st century will need to be constantly re-inventing themselves to surf the waves of change that globalized markets are creating. Why not start now to prepare for the likelihood that you will shift your professional focus multiple times across your working life? You may as well study what you find of interest, and remember to always keep an eye out for changes in the market that may signal possible employment opportunities for you.

Once you are out of school, no one is going to tell you what to study or what to learn. And it is totally up to you whether you want to learn about one or more new things, which means it is in your control. Everyday, you decide who you are going to be, and what you are going to know about, so make good choices and **Carpe Diem** (Latin for *Seize the Day*.)

Cultivate Your Critical Thinking Skills

As I wrote at the beginning of this Guide, there are no guarantees that even really smart people will get jobs that pay them to continue to learn and to think. You want to be one of those people, and you want to have a long successful career, so just as you will need to constantly reinforce your ability to *learn to learn* across multiple fields, you also need to continue to *cultivate your capacity for critical thinking*.

Thinking is a skill that, like a muscle, needs to be regularly strengthened.

If you want to maintain and deepen your ability to think critically and creatively, you need to practice thinking! It may sound silly, or obvious, but you really do need to pro-actively make yourself think and learn. Academics will tell you that to develop your critical thinking ability, you need to give yourself the opportunity to delve deeply—and for a long time—into a subject. You will literally increase your brainpower by thinking hard about subjects that do not come easily to you.

It can be challenging to closely read material that is new and difficult. As you read, examine and evaluate the claims made by the authors, as well as the evidence they provide to support their claims. Question assumptions, test hypotheses and develop your own well-reasoned arguments to support your ideas.

Thinking critically doesn't mean *being* critical in the sense of being negative about something. Instead, it means using your brainpower to discover essential truths, to discern crucial differences, and to recognize important facts and features.

Here are some good questions to have in your toolkit for critical thinking projects, especially good for work assignments but really, for all your critical thinking:

Start with the "who questions":
- Who benefits? Who is harmed or most directly affected?
- Who should you talk to about this? Who have you heard talk about it?
- Who will be the key people involved? Who will make the decision(s)?
- Who will deserve recognition for this?

Then turn to the "what questions":
- What are the strengths and weaknesses of a proposed action?
- What is the best/worse case scenario?
- What is another perspective? What is another alternative?
- What would be a counter-argument?
- What are the most important factors in the situation? The least?
- What can I or we do to make a positive change?
- What is getting in the way of action?

Cultivate your ability to be *objective*. Critical thinking depends on your ability to contextualize what you are learning and analyze its truth or its relevance from as objective — and *non emotional* — a point of view as is humanly possible. Humans are naturally emotional creatures, and it takes discipline to set aside our emotions and use reason to make decisions. Critical thinking in support of learning and decision-making succeeds when we can objectively and dispassionately analyze what an author is telling us, using reason, logic and evidence.

Practice Thinking Outside the Box

The expression "think outside the box" is a cliché by now, but it is a cliché with a lot of power: namely, *the person who can be creative and offer new ideas is often recognized and rewarded with more opportunities and more money.* Thinking creatively can obviously help you succeed at work, and it can also help you succeed at almost anything you attempt to do, so learning to think creatively is an excellent habit to cultivate.

But how can you learn to think creatively? There are many strategies for generating new ideas. One very powerful idea is to approach a problem *obliquely*, which means that rather than tackling the problem head on, you work on it indirectly. Here are some suggestions for how you can generate new and *oblique approaches* to problem solving:

- **Think in Pictures**

  Many people can envision connections better if they are drawn out with boxes and circles and arrows—if you can picture the business process flow, you can better identify and understand the bottlenecks.

- **Approach the Problem from the "Wrong" Place**

  Think of the worst things that you could do to solve your problem (the "wrong" answers) and then look for insights from why they are wrong.

- **Learn from Others**

  Apply strategies that work in one context to similar or analogous problems in a different domain.

- **Combine Unrelated Ideas to Generate New Ones**

  Einstein was famous for saying that "We cannot solve our problems with the same thinking we used when we created them." He advocated the use of "combinatory play" to open up one mental channel by dabbling in another. He would play the violin when he took a break from working on physics problems—and new approaches to physics would emerge in his mind while he played music.

- **Question Assumptions**

  As you approach a problem, write down (name) the many assumptions that you or your team are bringing to the table. Then challenge those assumptions—imagine they are 100% wrong, for example—how does that impact your analysis?

- **Ask Simple Questions**

  Critical and creative thinking are similar in some ways: asking simple questions can lead to unexpected insights. Ask yourself how this situation or problem is similar to others you've encountered. Ask what might happen if you change the assumptions slightly. Ask yourself about the timing and if it might be an option to do nothing about the problem—sometimes problems resolve themselves.

- **Be Attentive**

  Sometimes things go awry in ways that can be inspirational—the unexpected feedback or surprising result can jumpstart a creative insight on your problem

- **And Most Importantly, Write Things Down**

  You will generate many hundreds of ideas over your lifetime, more than you will likely ever use and more than you could ever keep in your head. *Write things down* in personal notebooks or online files. Keep track of the myriad things that interest you and over time, you will likely start to make some unexpected connections. Finding relationships and creating bridges between the most diverse ideas is a kind of everyday genius...so start cultivating your capacity to make unusual connections now, and you will reap the rewards later in life.

7. Cultivate Your Non-Cognitive Skills and Character traits

Developing the following specific character strengths and habits will make a significant contribution to your success, and to your financial stability and upward mobility:

- Perseverance/persistence, industriousness, grit, resilience, self-control
- Adaptability, curiosity, creativity, empathy, open-mindedness
- Future orientation, delay of gratification
- Self-discipline, impulse control, time management

Self-respect is the key to maintaining a productive and positive attitude toward yourself and your career, and **personal persistence is at the heart of self-respect**.

You need to wake up everyday and go to work and do your best work, no matter what is going on around you. If you do this, no matter what happens in an employment situation, you will maintain your self-respect and continue to strengthen your skills and your employability.

Anyone can find themselves in a situation where they are treated poorly, where the job conditions deteriorate due to bad bosses or bad colleagues or even bad clients. When this happens, successful people don't wait for the situation to become intolerable: even as they take whatever steps they can to try to improve the situation, they ramp up their networking and start to actively—though *confidentially*—look around for new opportunities. They do this because they are ambitious, of course, but also because they have a healthy self-respect that will not let them tolerate self-negating employment conditions.

What steps can you take to deepen your self-respect and build these important non-cognitive skills and character traits?

The following are basic steps to take, over and over, as you journey forward, but they are not magic bullets. There will be times when you are not prepared for a lay-off and all of a sudden find yourself job hunting. There will be times when you take a job only to find that it is not a good fit, or the company or the team or the manager is not what you thought it was, or what they promised it would be.

- **Be Mindful**

  Build self-discipline strengthening routines into your days. For example, if you get a very big sweet caffeinated drink at an expensive café every morning, try skipping it every other day. This practice of deliberate self-denial will help you **strengthen your will power and save money**. It will build your capacity for postponing gratification, which is a key attribute of all the most successful people.

  - *Put the money you save into an envelope and then into a savings account, or use it to buy some shares in a company you admire.*

- **Use Positive Self-Talk**

  Frequently remind yourself of past successes, and even try developing your own mantra that you can use to strengthen your sense of wellbeing. Tell yourself: "If I got through [past tough situation] I can definitely get through this." Use your experiences overcoming early challenges to reinforce your sense that you are a strong, creative, smart person who can figure things out for yourself.

- *Many people put Post-its all over their homes with inspirational words, mantras, and personal encouragement to remind them to think positively.*

- **Be Curious**

  Cultivate your sense of curiosity. Start by writing down a few questions you have about your field, or about other subjects related (or unrelated) to the work that you are doing. Tackle one or more questions each day, through Google searching or by asking people around you for their experience with the subject. As you get in the habit of questioning, you will find yourself learning more and more about a diverse array of subjects.

  - *Learning how to ask good questions, and learning how to listen to the answers, is a critical skill for success in any field.*

- **Find Kindred Spirits**

  Follow the trails of the ideas that interest you the most, reading widely and continuing to enhance your understanding. Amazingly, the more you do this, and the more you learn about different subjects, *the more interesting you will become to other people.* Also, as you invest time and energy into subjects that fascinate you, the more likely it is that you will find *kindred spirits* in the world, people who share your fascination with that subject. Finding people with similar interests will improve your quality of life, widen your social network, and offer you unexpected opportunities to learn and have fun.

  - *You never know what activity or which acquaintance will make an important career connection for you!*

- **Be Respectful**

  The original Golden Rule is to treat others as you would have them treat you. Follow this advice and offer everyone, from receptionists to couriers to colleagues and bosses, the respect that you would like them to give you. If you maintain this habit throughout your career, you will make allies and friends, and no matter how bad things get at work, you will have someone you can laugh with. It is remarkable how helpful a good laugh with colleagues can be when work gets stressful and crazy.

By cultivating your personal capacity to persevere in the face of difficulty you will deepen your self-respect, and you will be better able to deal with difficult people and overcome difficult situations.

8. Learn to Accept Feedback and Course Correct

One of life's most important lessons is that we need to learn how to graciously accept feedback and take the time to process the information we are given by others. If we are lucky enough to have people in our lives who will give us honest personal feedback, we need to be open to hearing what they have to say, and express our thanks to them when they do share their impressions with us.

Unfortunately, with the exception of professional feedback on our work performance (more on that below,) it is actually pretty rare to have anyone take the time to tell you something about how you have interacted with, or have been perceived, by others.

It turns out there is often a gap between how we think we are doing in the world and how we are really doing, and *it can be hard to improve if we don't know what's wrong.* Ironically, we often make the same mistakes over and over again since we don't have a good way to recognize what we are doing wrong in the first place.

How can you find helpful—and not hurtful—feedback outside of the work environment? Family and close friends who have your best interests at heart are likely the best sources of feedback when it comes to evaluating non-work behaviors.

When something happens in our lives that upsets us, or when we make a mistake—or feel that we have misjudged a situation but cannot figure out how we might have done better—it can be a good idea to ask a friend who is not involved in the situation to talk it through with you. Someone you trust, who has known you over time, is often able to point things out to you in a way that you can hear without taking offense, giving you a chance to think about the issue from a new perspective.

Everyone these days is talking about how important it is to fail, and emphasizing the life lessons we can learn from making mistakes. *The only way to learn from mistakes is to seriously reflect on why they were mistakes, and then to move forward recommitted to doing your best work.* Successful people do not give up when they make mistakes, but instead they take seriously the idea that they can learn from their own mistakes.

You will surely continue to make mistakes, but **your goal is to learn from your mistakes, and not to make the same mistake twice**.

Feedback at Work: Use Extreme Caution

Most employers offer yearly evaluations for their employees, and these annual reviews are usually tied to compensation reviews. A good performance review has traditionally been required in order to receive a raise. Some companies continue to operate this way, and for many people, once a year discussions with their supervisors to review their performance are quite sufficient.

New approaches to performance review and support include more frequent employee performance evaluation, such as

- snapshot or mini-reviews that can be done quickly,
- are not specifically tied to compensation, and
- which can even be requested by employees from their managers after big deals are closed or projects completed.

Whether once a year or more often, how can you get feedback that is helpful to you? HR professionals advise that it is a good strategy to be pro-active in the meeting and ask your reviewer:

- what was positive about my performance, and
- what could I do differently next time?

Every workplace is different, and as you move forward in your career you will receive feedback from a range of people who may—or may not—have your best interests at heart. While it is always a good idea to assume that the main goal of a performance review is to reward and reinforce those good habits that management sees as supportive of achieving the organization's objectives, that doesn't mean that you will always get supportive or even meaningful feedback from a supervisor or colleague. **No matter what you hear from a supervisor or colleague, positive or negative, you must be very cautious about what you say or reveal in response**.

The truth is, while you should be brutally honest *with yourself* about your performance at work, it is rarely, if ever, in your interest to reveal how you feel about your work product, how you feel about your work colleagues, or how you feel about the organization. For the most part, you should keep any self-criticism to yourself, and if you receive critical comments during a review, you should accept them without endorsing them.

Keep your cool no matter what anyone says to you—and don't argue with them about their observations. If you hear anything that is less than positive about your performance, just listen quietly and allow them to finish speaking. Don't attempt to refute their criticisms. Stay calm, and practice quiet breathing to prevent yourself from getting "hot under the collar," which can lead to angry, defensive or aggressive responses.

Every work environment is different, and, as you progress in your career, you may receive explicitly supportive coaching. Even when your supervisor or HR team is clearly working with you in an effort to drive your performance in support of your advancement within the company, it is still in your interest to hold your cards close to your chest and not to reveal too many personal details or feelings to them.

At the end of the day, remember that you are really "Me, Inc." and your employer's HR team doesn't work for you—they work for your employer, and your interests will not always align with theirs.

9. Build Resilience Through Relationships

One of the most effective ways to build your personal resilience is to put time and effort into sustaining your friendships and your relationships with family members. Not only is it great to have people to go out with and people to talk with, but you will strengthen your own interpersonal skills and empathic awareness as you share experiences and stories about life with your friends and family.

The ubiquitous computer technology that connects us can also be isolating, so it is important to plan time for in-person socializing with others. It is too easy to spend a few days in a row just working away at a computer monitor, followed by evenings spent alone, watching shows on your laptop. While it is great to communicate with friends through a mobile phone using FaceTime or other video chat services, be sure to schedule real dates where you and your friends can generate some lasting memories together! Your friends and family really do care about you, and if you neglect human relationships, there will be real costs in the long run.

Be aware of the danger of spending too much time worrying about professional advancement and recognition and somehow missing the moments of bliss, when you look around you and everything is…truly…OK. Things in your life may not be exactly as you pictured them, but if you are able to step away from your own expectations, you will usually be surprised to find that you have created something that is rich and rewarding and satisfying—*for the moment*. And the big take away lesson is that **the moment is all we really have**.

As the Zen masters of the East and the West tell us,
- "Every moment is a gift: that's why they call it the present." *Unknown*
- "Life is available only in the present moment. If you abandon the present moment you cannot live the moments of your daily life deeply." *Thich Nhat Hanh*
- "I have realized that the past and future are real illusions, that they exist in the present, which is what there is and all there is." *Alan Watts*

Golden Tip #26
You Are Not A Robot.

Only robots work 24/7. Take vacations, spend time with friends. No one can or should be always on, always networking, always seeking their next opportunity. There are going to be days, weeks and months when you should just do your job and create good work that impresses your supervisors and showcases your abilities.

Ironically, it turns out that one of the hardest things to develop is a capacity to *live in the moment* and yet it is only by doing so that we can make our lived experience truly memorable. If we spend all our time thinking about our to-do list and what we have planned for tomorrow or next week, or where we hope to travel next month, we deprive ourselves—and the people we are living and working with—of our presence in those moments. To really succeed at working with others requires that we give ourselves permission to *be real with them in real time,* to share the particular experiences that are available to us at that time and in that place.

"The most precious gift we can offer others is our presence. When mindfulness embraces those we love, they will bloom like flowers."

—*Thich Nhat Hanh*

Chapter Five Take-Aways

1. **You are what you repeatedly do.** Take Aristotle's wisdom to heart and watch out for the bad habits that we all fall prey to, especially when we are stressed.
2. **Don't badmouth past employers or colleagues.** It will not help you with future colleagues and could hurt you.
3. **Develop strong self-care habits**—they will keep you going when times get tough. And times get tough for everyone.
4. **Keep pushing yourself intellectually**—learn as much as you can about all the things that interest you. Cultivate your curiosity.
5. **Live in the moment**—it is all you really have.

6 | Creating Your Life, Not Just Your Career

Every life is a work of art—your personal adventure that you create, and re-create, as you live out your days on our planet. You are truly the star of your own movie, the choreographer of your private dance. Your career is one part of that story; an important part to be sure, but the totality of your existence—your life—is much more than your career.

Young people often feel overwhelmed by what they see as too many options and not enough clarity within themselves about their true professional calling in life. Over the course of this book I have advocated for **cultivating your own curiosity as a strategy** for interrogating your possible passions—and I truly believe that if you are curious, persistent and lucky, you should be able to find work that stimulates your mind and makes your heart sing.

You probably won't ever find the "perfect job." The best that most of us can do is to find the job that is "perfect for now." Every job will have its drawbacks along with its attractions. The goal is to find a job offering a wage that, at a minimum, covers your expenses and gives you room to grow—to grow your skills, your network, and your confidence in yourself.

In this concluding chapter I look at strategies for staying employable, being proactive so you can be lucky, and finding ways to bring it all together so that you can continue to be paid to think about the things that matter to you throughout your career and you can build a career—and a life—that you can be proud of.

Stay Relevant as the World of Work Automates

As you travel across the decades of your future career, you must continually drive yourself forward with the same energy and optimism that you project when you are young. Despite media speculation about a world where robots will do all the work, you need to remember that, in your career, you will be competing against other people for jobs, not against robots.

Robots will continue to spread throughout our society, aided by Artificial Intelligence systems that are becoming more and more sophisticated. Staying relevant and competitive in the world—no matter what your profession—will increasingly require *Emotional Intelligence* as well as a capacity to *learn how to learn* so you can navigate the new technologies and new systems you will undoubtedly encounter.

Here are three steps you can take to ensure that you stay relevant and competitive for new opportunities:

- **Continually hone your interpersonal skills**, be honest with yourself, and try to learn from your mistakes. If you follow this life-long learning path, your *Emotional Intelligence* will increase as you gain experience working with different kinds of people, you will work more effectively and you will increase your chances of promotion to more challenging opportunities.
- **Invest in your thinking skills.** Read books and take courses that are intellectually challenging to ensure that you don't get in a rut. Employers are going to be offering even more on-the-job training and will be expecting employees to up-skill on demand, placing even more of a premium on the ability to quickly process new information and develop new skills.
- **Cultivate valuable skills and personality traits** such as self-direction, drive, self-discipline, critical thinking, creativity, emotional intelligence, adaptability and a capacity for collaboration.

Keep Yourself Employable:
Schedule Regular Self Reviews

Employers are not the only ones who should get to review you! In fact, it's a great idea to conduct your own performance/career review several times a year, to take an honest look at what you are doing to advance in your career.

- Are you where you expected to be in terms of the challenges you face in your job? Are you stretching out of your comfort zone to take on new challenges?
- Are you expanding and strengthening your personal and professional networks?
- Are you using your existing skills as well as learning new skills?
- Are you maintaining and strengthening your online presence through blogging, posting comments and otherwise managing your digital footprint?
- Very importantly, are you documenting your work projects and keeping your resume and portfolio up to date/ in top shape?

Be sure to keep copies of good writing projects so that you can use them as writing samples, and keep track of any classes you take or certificates you earn, so that if you need to show your preparation for a new task at work or even apply for a new job, you can easily document where and when you got the relevant training.

Reach Out For Support

Sometimes it can be incredibly valuable to get a different perspective on a work situation. For example, you may need reassurance and guidance when it seems like your career progression has stalled. Or, you may seek tactical advice when faced with a political challenge regarding colleagues at work.

Use Your Inner Circle as a Sounding Board

Ask trustworthy members of your inner circle, in confidence, for advice on work challenges and opportunities.

Keep family and close family friends apprised of your career progress, so they can offer you relevant advice when you need it.

Continue to Build Your Personal Board of Directors

Cultivate relationships with some of your professional colleagues and supervisors. As you progress through different jobs and organizations, there may be colleagues, supervisors and others with whom you really connect at a level that is deeper than just professional acquaintance. Over time, if you cultivate these relationships, you will build a wonderful sounding board of people who really know your professional capacity and who can be mentors and guides for you throughout your career.

Even if you are lucky enough to have knowledgeable relatives who can be good advisors to you as you advance in your career, you should still build a personal board of directors for "Me, Inc." that includes people who can not only advise you but who can be professional references for you.

*Remember: it is not considered appropriate for family or family friends to offer professional references for you, though it is fine for them to offer a professional **referral** connecting you to someone in their circle or industry.*

Helping Others Will Help You Succeed

One of the most powerful strategies for increasing your social capital is to ask people "how can I help you?" You may think that you don't have any way to help older, more powerful or more well-placed people, but that isn't true, and anyway, it's always a good idea to try to help others. The expression "what goes around, comes around" is a good mantra to keep in mind: by offering to help other people, for example by offering to introduce people through LinkedIn, or suggesting people for jobs and opportunities such as board positions, you insert yourself into others' consciousness as a helpful person, which can only be good for you over the long run.

Helping those around you can also be as simple as listening to them and being there for them when they need a friend. It can be more, too, of course: for example, you can help edit a cover letter, do a mock interview or be an audience for a friend practicing her elevator speech. Over time, it becomes a habit, when you meet new people, to explore the social and professional overlaps you may have and brainstorm how you might be able to help each other.

By connecting on LinkedIn, each of you can browse the others' contacts to see if there is someone you'd like to be introduced to. This is the brilliance of social networking, where you are each individually and simultaneously building your own social capital and also creating a bond that might grow into a personal or professional friendship.

Being Authentic

As you build your personal and professional network, be mindful of how you come across to people, and seek, whenever possible, to share your authentic, trustworthy self with those you meet. You can't control how others perceive you. How you choose to present yourself will impact their perception, so be self-aware and try to have some idea of how you are coming across to people.

Golden Tip #27
You Get What You Give.

Is the glass half full or half empty? Are you an optimist or a pessimist? However you feel about the world, remember that when you are interacting with people, they see and react to what you show them. If you offer a positive outlook on life, a can-do attitude, and a smile, you will generally get a better response than if you scowl and present yourself as critical, disappointed or disillusioned.

Think about your posture, your facial expressions and your vocabulary—and not only when you are in an interview situation or meeting with professors. When I said in **Chapter One** to *be yourself* I meant *be your best self*, the one who can project your emotions and thoughts with an authentic style that reflects your true personality and which will draw others to you.

Your goal is to build trust with others who are (hopefully) sharing their true selves with you. If you are shy, or introverted, or insecure that others may not like you, you probably already know that you need to take small steps each day to build your confidence. If you are confident with your friends but get quiet in groups where you don't know anyone well, then you need to widen the spheres of activity where you can feel confident by stepping outside of your comfort zone. Join new groups to meet new people...who will become your friends or, if not friends, at least people you can interact with in a confident way.

At the very least, you should cultivate an open, honest way of speaking one-on-one, so that even if you are not well known to lots of people, those who do know you feel that they know and can trust the real you.

Be Authentic, But Not Careerist: Some ambitious people can seem to be *careerist*—that is, focused only how others can help them. You should strive to be *authentic*—that is, able to pursue your objectives in a way that shows you understand there is more at stake in life than your own success.

An *authentic* person acknowledges that she is part of a larger effort and speaks with humility about her role, recognizing that she is contributing to a team project *and that the opportunity to continue to do so is not guaranteed.*

Golden Tip #28
Remember ABC:
Be Authentic, Be a Builder,
Be a Collaborator.

Being authentic in the context of work means talking the talk and walking the walk of a *builder and collaborator* who respects the contributions of others. One mark of a team player is that they never take all the credit for the work of their group—they talk about *our efforts* and *our success.*

Avoiding Careerism

All the networking in the world will not help you if the people you meet don't like you for some reason. Now, I am not saying that everyone you meet should fall in love with you, but I am saying that you should make efforts to be genuine and avoid coming across to people as a *user*—that is, as someone who has a *transactional* approach to people. The opposite of transactional is **relational**; the lesson is that you should *always approach connecting with others as an opportunity to create relationships, not transactions.*

When you reach out to meet new people for informational interviews, be very conscious that you are asking them for some of their time. Time is valuable, so be sure you don't waste it by being unprepared or asking generic questions—the answers to which you could have found on their company bio or LinkedIn profile.

Most importantly, approach each new informational interview with humility and gracious appreciation. Be sure that you are not following a script of just Q & A. Try to listen thoughtfully to the remarks that the other person is making and offer interesting replies. Build the conversation around their remarks, linking them to your questions as appropriate.

Avoiding careerism is more than avoiding strictly Q & A during info interviews; it also means learning when to hold back, and not press someone for information and advice. Ideally, you are networking into social and professional circles where you will have more than one chance to encounter people. In a perfect world, you might be introduced to someone and you both light up and say "Hi, didn't we meet before at XYZ event?" And that can lead to a warm exchange and a plan to meet up again in the future. It might be that you run into someone several times before you exchange cards or have a real conversation.

Driving Your Career Forward

The most successful people seem to have an effortless trajectory to their career arcs, but when you talk with them, they will often express surprise at how their professional lives worked out, and they will almost always mention luck as well as what might have seemed like off-beat choices early on. They will frame their narratives positively, and they will usually express awe at how lucky they have been. Certainly they will have been lucky, but it's likely that they have been very hardworking and prepared for opportunity as well…as you can be, too!

Catch the Luck: It is absolutely true that chance encounters have a way of changing your life—you never know who you will meet on an elevator, at the gym working out, or at a lecture offered by your alumni association. The key to "catching the luck" in these chance encounters is to be open-minded, easy going and friendly, and to follow up appropriately.

Be Authentic and Relatable: Many people are naturally *ingratiating,* which means "capable of winning favor" and "intended or adopted in order to gain approval or favor." If it seems calculating, ingratiating behavior can be taken as *sycophantic,* which describes a person who praises powerful people to get their approval—which is definitely *not* positive. Your goal is to be *authentic and relatable,* and you want people to like you for who you are, not for what you say to them that makes them feel good or powerful.

Learn From Mistakes: Everyone makes mistakes. Everyone. Successful people don't necessarily make fewer mistakes, though that may be a part of why they are successful. **Successful people learn from their mistakes and do not make the same mistake twice.** By the way, mistakes are not the same as "failures." These days, the business press is filled with advice to technology entrepreneurs about "failing fast and often" but with respect to your career, you should not call your mistakes failures. Why? Because naming your experience is a part of your self-talk, and associating the word failure with yourself is like drinking poison: it will hurt you and it will not help you learn from your mistakes.

Be Self Aware: Proud + Humble, Confident + Open Minded

As people grow older they should become more mature about life and work, and this maturity should translate into and accompany the habits of mind and behavior that you are learning from this book. Youthful arrogance—if any—should be tempered over time, and you should strive to be someone whom others will say "gets it"—which is a short hand compliment offered to describe a person who understands what's really going on in a workplace, or in life.

Consider Your Circumstances of Birth a Reality Check, Not a Limit

No matter what the circumstances of a person's birth, if they apply themselves in school, work hard in life, and have a little bit of good luck, there is no limit to what they can accomplish. Most people believe this, and for good reason: it is still mostly true that if a person invests enough time and energy in school and in continued skills training, they will find a path forward that allows them to make a decent living and build a rewarding life.

I am not saying that there aren't obstacles in life, and I am not saying that the world is fair—*it is not fair*, and there will always be some people born with more or different advantages than others. Those advantages may include family resources such as money, an abundance of loving kindness, confidence building support or relentless pushing to succeed, or the advantages might be innate talents such as perfect pitch or a photographic memory.

It is important to remember that even the most advantaged people suffer and make mistakes; it's just that money and family resources are a cushion that helps people bounce back from bad choices or bad luck. If, like most of us, you have to make your way in the world without some of those advantages, then it just makes sense to embrace the challenge and be proud of your hard won successes in life.

Golden Tip #30
Don't Let Fear Sabotage You.
Everyone has insecurities about presenting themselves as an expert—everyone suffers at one time or another from so-called *imposter syndrome*. It is important to face the future without fear so you can find the inner strength to face challenges and seize opportunities when they present themselves. Over time, you will become more confident as you live and work in the world. As the Nike slogan says, *Just Do It.*

Whatever the circumstances of your birth, the evidence is clear that the choices you make can help you get ahead in the world—or can hurt your chances of success. Since you are old enough to read this Guide, you have certainly already been affected by the choices that others have made for you, as well as by the choices you yourself have made.

The challenge going forward is to be sure that you are making good choices and that you *do not let setbacks beat you down*.

Each morning offers a brand new day, so remember: whatever you have been doing (or not doing) doesn't matter—the important thing is how you think and act going forward. And you will probably find, over the course of your life, that you will need to re-invent yourself multiple times, taking stock of where you are and what you need to make happen for yourself so you can be happy and fulfilled.

Make the most of your assets. The social class you were born into, the social and financial capital you and your family can command, and the educational resources available to you are all significant influences on your likely career trajectory. Your objective should be to make the most of these assets.

Finally, it is helpful to recall that everyone has to play the hand they are dealt when it comes to the life lottery, and even those who appear to have won that contest by being born into wealth and privilege may not have the love and support they need to build a happy and productive life.

There is a critical link between perseverance, success and self-respect, and many individuals who appear to have family or wealth advantages *actually fail to succeed or are otherwise unhappy in their lives because they haven't developed the character traits of happy, successful people.*

Do not let the circumstances of your birth become an excuse for not trying your best, and be sure to celebrate whatever and whoever strengthened and enriched you and helped you get to where you are today. Be proud of yourself, but not too proud to have some humility: a positive, humble attitude and a smile will open doors you never even knew existed.

Career and Life Arcs

As you grow older, you may worry that you are losing momentum if you are not being promoted quickly, or if you are not regularly advancing in salary and title by moving from company to company. In your life — outside of the office — you may start a household with another person, buy real estate, have children…and begin to value stability more than you feel the need to seek out new challenges.

Whatever your life path, the fact is that most people need to work and earn money for many decades — and therefore, they need to *find ways to balance and integrate their professional and their personal ambitions over their entire life*. For many people, their life arc will necessarily include periods of time when they are emphasizing home, family, education, hobby or other interests — and perhaps not earning as much money or seeking out new professional challenges. And that's perfectly ok!

All people struggle, on a daily basis, to fit in time for exercise, to choose the healthy lunch option, to spend quality time with friends and family. When you are trying to do all the right things personally and professionally, and yet you don't seem to be able to find the right next challenge, it can feel incredibly overwhelming. It can be so frustrating that you may begin to feel defeated.

Golden Tip #31
Dysfunctional Organizations Defeat People.
It is a universally recognized rule of business life that when a *highly functional person meets a dysfunctional organization, the organization wins*. Don't take it personally — as soon as you realize the problem, decide to learn whatever you can in the situation and get yourself a new job as quickly as you can!

In those moments, you need to remind yourself that **your life is more than just your career**. While it is important to be focused and driven about your career, it is also very important to take a long view. Sometimes you just need to step back and consolidate your gains so that you will be prepared for the next push forward. Sometimes you need to rest and recharge your batteries, and sometimes you need to take care of other people in your life—your parents, siblings, partners and children.

A career is essentially a 40+ year marathon. There will be periods of time—years, even—when it may seem like you are running in place and not really moving forward, even as time is passing. There will be years when you are not even running—that is, you may step out of the career marathon to do other things with your time.

It is totally up to you how you narrate this to yourself and to others.

Framing and re-framing your story of your career will underlie how you create meaning from, transform and cope with the ups and downs of everyday life. The career piece is just one part of the much larger story of your life, albeit an important piece. A person who neglects the human connections in their life and focuses only on personal ambition and getting ahead may have what looks like a successful career—but they will miss out on life's greatest experiences. It is famously remarked that "no one, on their deathbed, says they wished they had spent more time at the office."

Do what you can to create a healthy integration of work and life, and really let yourself appreciate the satisfaction to be found in everyday successes.

Have confidence that, over time, your career will offer you the challenges you seek as well as the rewards you deserve.

Having It All

When you are just starting out, it can be quite overwhelming to think about the life choices ahead of you, and there has been a lot written about the challenges of combining a successful career with a fulfilling family life. It's pretty clear that modern life is very stressful and some organizations and some jobs just don't make it easy to be a parent or an attentive partner.

If you have a well-paid job, you can provide a comfortable living for yourself and your family, but many of the highest paying jobs require that you work many more hours than you might want—hours that you could be spending with your family and friends. So there is an inevitable trade-off—and there is a significant risk that if you prioritize work over life in a way that is truly imbalanced, you may be disappointed when your career plateaus, you lose a job for no good reason, or you just come to the end of your working life and find yourself adrift without a meaningful sense of community.

The life arc that you create for yourself will reflect your assets, opportunities and efforts—and you don't do yourself any favors by denying your agency in it all. After all, we do make choices in life; we do decide to pursue some chances and not others. It is mentally healthy to face up to—to own—your life decisions, even as you recognize that many aspects of your life situation are not in your control. How you define success for yourself will surely change over time, and your experiences—good and bad—will color how you perceive your overall career achievement.

Having it all is really a series of layered challenges:
- There is a layer that is about money vs time,
- There is a layer that is about doing honorable work that you feel helps make the world a better place vs work that you do to pay the bills but which doesn't make your heart sing, and
- There is a layer that is about integrating work and life to create both financially and emotionally rewarding experiences.

Everyone is constantly examining and re-examining their approaches to these challenges and, over the course of your career, the balances will surely shift. When you are just starting out in the work world, it is appropriate to prioritize your career ambitions. Later on, it may be desirable to step away from a demanding role.

Making a Difference

If you look around at the opportunities to earn a living, you will quickly see that the salaries associated with different sectors vary.

- For-profit commercial firms tend to pay their employees the highest salaries,
- Academic/think tank and government roles are usually well compensated but not at the rate of for-profits, and
- Nonprofit organizations' salaries tend to be low—though salary levels depend on the size and funding of the nonprofit.

I truly understand the desire to make a living doing work that you believe is helping to *make a difference*—that is, work that will contribute to finding solutions to the world's problems. As you find your own way in the world, there are times when you must choose between less-than-perfect job options. *The important thing is to be clear with yourself about what you are doing, and why.* All work that supports life and family is honorable, and as long as you are honest about your motivations and evaluate your options carefully, you will find a decent path to follow.

There are more and more ways to do well and do good in our world. For example, as discussed in **Chapter Four**, there are *social entrepreneurs* solving pressing problems using insights gleaned from behavioral economics along with innovative outreach and implementation methods, including new digital technologies. As digital natives move up the ranks of all our organizations, we can expect to see more and more innovation in idea generation and service delivery in both the public and private sectors.

As noted earlier, the world is not fair—and it is not fair on many levels. Even as we must embrace the fight for a fairer and more environmentally sustainable world, we also must face the realities of our own circumstances. Everyone has a different set of stresses—some people are caring for older relatives at the same time that they have their own young children and busy careers, some people have no financial cushion when unexpected expenses arise, some people face personal medical challenges that compromise and complicate their ability to pursue their careers. Everyone has something.

On the airplanes, when the flight attendants are explaining the emergency procedures, they tell you to put your oxygen mask on before turning to help a person near you—and the same logic applies to life and career.

You cannot give much to others—whether time, energy or money— if you are struggling on those fronts yourself.

It helps to keep in mind that the fight for social, economic and environmental justice has many dimensions, and over time, *you can find ways to be part of the solution to the challenges you care about if you stay intentional* and keep an open mind as you continually widen your circles through networking, networking and networking.

It is valuable—and validating—to think broadly about the sum of all your activities, including where you volunteer your time, which groups you support with your personal philanthropy, and how you raise your children (if you have them) to be good people in the world. You can contribute money and time to many different organizations over the course of your lifetime. If/when you find yourself working in a lucrative job that is not overtly focused on solving social or environmental problems, then that is a good time to find a nonprofit to engage with as a board member or contributor.

In summary, the most helpful way to think about *having it all* is to define it as a challenge you will strive to meet over your entire lifetime. It's a well known sentiment (variously attributed to Madeleine Albright, Betty Friedan, or Oprah Winfrey) that "you can have it all, just not at the same time." Remember that your life and your career will always add up to much more than merely the job you do for money at one particular period of your life.

Getting Paid to Think + Thinking About Things that Matter to You

At the start of this book I noted that the world is very competitive and that even the smartest among us don't always get the chance to be paid to think about challenging and interesting subjects that we care about. The point of this book has been to help you develop the **habits of mind and behavior** that will give you the best chance of achieving that objective as you progress in your career.

Many people describe graduating from college and starting their careers as a scary time. On the one hand, it seems like there are many different possible paths to follow and at the same time, the possible career alternatives seem to recede quickly from view as daily life, post-college, gets underway. How can it be that before you graduate you can do anything and just a year or two afterwards, it seems like you could be stuck doing something you don't like, or worse, be un- or underemployed?

The truth is that many people get to the end of college, finish their majors—whatever they were—and only then start to think about what they really are interested in doing with their lives. If they studied a subject that has a clear career trajectory, they might go for an entry-level job in that field only to discover that they are bored to tears by it. And if they studied something that doesn't have a clear career trajectory, they face the prospect of taking whatever job they can find out of college and trying to figure it out from there.

I guarantee you that the vast majority of college educated students, whether they have studied STEM subjects or were humanities/liberal arts majors, will find jobs after college that utilize at least some aspect of their education and skill set. College graduates are able to offer firms analytical thinking, clear writing, and a capacity to process information that reflects their ability to get through college coursework.

The biggest career challenge you will face in your life is the need to define, and then redefine, what really matters to you intellectually. Only you can know what you want to think about and who you really want to work with.

It is very hard to know, when you are in your twenties, what your career trajectory will look like when you reflect on it from an older vantage point. You cannot predict what life opportunities you will have, nor even what you will be interested in among the myriad of interesting subjects there are to study and learn about.

But you can work steadily on projects that enlarge your base of knowledge and enrich your skill set. And you can cultivate your curiosity, and invest time and effort in exploring familiar subjects as well as subjects that are new and interesting to you.

If you implement the **habits of mind and behavior** that I have described in this book, you should, over time, achieve a steady growth in opportunities to be paid to think about things that matter to you. You should also continue to gain new knowledge and learn new skills, and, if you are lucky, find career satisfaction along with a balanced and happy life filled with friends and family.

You will make a difference in the world through your choices: choices about subjects to become expert in and issues to care about, choices about the types of people, companies and nonprofit organizations you will associate yourself with, and choices about how you will invest your time and money.

Make good choices!

RF | Notes and Additional Reading

Chapter One

- Early versions of some of this material appeared in handouts I wrote and edited with the career services team at the University of Chicago's Harris School of Public Policy.
- In re: how to search/connect with people in different industries: Jordan Phoenix http://uncommonsense.is/brainfood
- In re: Networking advice https://www.usnews.com/topics/author/arnie-fertig
- ***There is Life After College: What Parents and Students Should Know About Navigating School to Prepare for the Jobs of Tomorrow.*** By Jeffrey J. Selingo [2016, William Morrow/HarperCollins]

Chapter Two

- In re: digital footprints: https://medium.com/broken-window/a-complete-guide-to-keeping-your-digital-identity-short-and-sweet-570cfb3c2ed4#.n0jsqmyap
- ***Graduate to a Great Career: How Smart Students, New Graduates, and Young Professionals can Launch BRAND YOU.*** By Catherine Kaputa [2016, Nicholas Brealey]

Chapter Three

- In re: Resume writing—Creating Your Dream Job Resume by Carol Crosby https://blog.nafsa.org/2015/05/04/creating-your-dream-job-resume/
- In re: Alternative Credentials https://www.insidehighered.com/news/2017/09/14/feds-release-data-nondegree-credentials-including-certificates-and-licenses?utm_source=Inside+Higher+Ed&utm_campaign=70b526824e-DNU20170914&utm_medium=email&utm_term=0_1fc-bc04421-70b526824e-198469381&mc_cid=70b526824e&mc_eid=db23fd929f
- ***Kiss, Bow, or Shake Hands.*** By Terri Morrison and Wayne A. Conaway [2006, F&W Media, Inc.]

Chapter Four

- *The New Rules of Work: The Modern Playbook for Navigating Your Career.* By Alexandra Cavoulacos and Kathryn Minshew [2017, Penguin Random House]
- *The Career Playbook: Essential Advice for Today's Aspiring Young Professional.* By James M. Citrin [2015, Penguin Random House].

Chapter Five

- In re: thinking creatively/obliquely http://www.liquidagency.com/brand-exchange/rule-9-approach-answers-obliquely//
- In re: critical thinking—https://chroniclevitae.com/news/1691-what-is-critical-thinking-anyway?cid=gn&utm_source=gn&utm_medium=en&elqTrackId=e2341b9ea10a47d49f19f-81b2e65092f&elq=dfb74c31d5774eae9ff0ecf48ee15857&elqaid=12498&elqat=1&elqCampaignId=5095#sthash.f7RNtDGf.dpuf
- In re: Elon Musk and Thinking Across Disciplines—Michael Simmons, "How Elon Musk Learns Faster and Better than Everyone Else"—https://medium.com/@michaeldsimmons/how-elon-musk-learns-faster-and-better-than-everyone-else-a010a4f586ef
- *I am That Girl.* By Alexis Jones [2014, Evolve, Publishing]
- *Blind Spots: The Ten Business Myths you Can't Afford to Believe on Your Path to Success.* By Alexandra Levit [2011, Berkley Books]
- *The Go-Getter Girl's Guide.* By Debra Shigley [2009 St. Martin's Press]

Chapter Six

- *Work, Pause, Thrive.* By Lisen Stromberg [2017, BenBella Books, Inc]
- *Designing Your Life.* By Bill Burnett and Dave Evans [2016 Knopf]
- *Composing A Life.* By Mary Catherine Bateson [2001 Grove Press]

International Students

- *The International Advantage: Get Noticed. Get Hired.* By Marcelo Barros [2015, Barros]
- *Power Ties: The International Student's Guide to Finding A Job in the United States – Revised and Updated.* By Dan Beaudry [2014, CreateSpace]
- *Make Your American Dream A Reality: How To Find a Job As An International Student in the United States.* By Ceren Cubukcu [2013, CS Publishing]

RF | Internet Sites

This **Resource File** offers links to a wide variety of sites offering job postings and other information that may be helpful as you explore possible career paths. Be sure to type the URL into your browser as written and be cautious about sharing your personal information with commercial sites. This is not an exhaustive list but should be helpful as you get started!

Check in regularly with your campus career services team, as there are likely to be upcoming visits to your campus by some employers, and they may have other personal contacts at employers that can be helpful to you as you begin your search.

General Career Resources

U.S. Department of Labor, Bureau of Labor Statistics

- **Occupational Outlook Handbook.** Provides information on careers from an occupational perspective along with industry nature, working conditions, employment, occupations in the industry, training and advancement, earnings and benefits, employment outlook, and lists of organizations that can provide additional information. http://www.bls.gov/ooh/
- **Overview of BLS statistics by industry.** Comprehensive site including profiles of the nine major industry divisions. Each profile contains industry facts and employment, hours, earnings, and a wealth of other data. http://www.bls.gov/bls/industry.htm

Career One Stop

A site where you can explore additional training and education opportunities and learn about negotiating for Salary and Benefits across professions.

- http://www.careeronestop.org/FindTraining/find-training.aspx?&frd=true
- http://www.careeronestop.org/JobSearch/Interview/negotiate-your-salary.aspx?&frd=true
- International students can get current Visa advice http://www.myvisajobs.com

You can review these sites to find for-profit and non-profit organizations' financial data:

- https://finance.yahoo.com/lookup - commercial firms
- https://www.google.com/finance - commercial firms
- http://www.wsj.com/public/page/companyresearch.html - Wall Street Journal
- http://www2.guidestar.org/Home.aspx - Searchable directory of nonprofit organizations; data includes location, contact, number of employees/volunteers, revenue, program areas.

You can explore salary information at these sites:

- www.salary.com
- www.payscale.com
- http://www.glassdoor.com/index.htm

Job Boards

General/Private Sector

- http://www.indeed.com/
- https://www.linkedin.com/
- https://www.simplyhired.com
- http://www.americasjobexchange.com/
- http://us.jobs/
- http://monster.com

NonProfit/Philanthropy

- Idealist: Job board focused on nonprofit and NGO jobs. http://www.idealist.org/
- NPO.net: http://www.npo.net/
- Community Career Center: http://www.nonprofitjobs.org/
- InterAction NGO: https://ngojobboard.org/
- Public Service Careers: http://publicservicecareers.org/
- Work For Good: https://www.workforgood.org/
- Chronicle of Philanthropy: https://philanthropy.com
- Philanthropy New York: https://philanthropynewyork.org
- Philanthropy News Digest: http://philanthropynewsdigest.org/jobs
- The Chronicle of Higher Education: https://chroniclevitae.com/job_search/new
- Bridgespan Group: http://www.bridgespan.org/Nonprofit_Jobs.aspx

- Common Good Careers: http://commongoodcareers.org/
- Opportunities in Public Affairs: http://www.opajobs.com/
- Public Affairs Council: http://pac.org/jobs

United States and Local Government

General Information

- USAjobs: Official government information. https://www.usajobs.gov/
- GoGovernment: Resources on how to find and apply for government jobs. http://gogovernment.org/
- Workforce Recruitment Program for College Students with Disabilities (WRP): Government and private sector employment. http://www.dol.gov/odep/wrp/
- The Best Places to Work in the Federal Government: Annual ranking of government agencies by employee satisfaction, innovation and leadership. http://bestplacestowork.org/BPTW/index.php
- Partnership for Public Service: Designed to help students learn about government work; useful links to agencies and job information. http://ourpublicservice.org/
- Non government but in Washington D.C: The Center for Internships and Academic Affairs: http://www.twc.edu/

Selected Federal Agencies

- US Office of Personnel Management: Job seekers for the Federal Government. http://www.opm.gov/
- Congressional Budget Office: Fellowships, internships, full-time jobs, FAQs, and other information about the CBO. http://www.cbo.gov/about/careers
- House of Representatives: Positions with house members and committees, and other congressional organizations. http://www.house.gov/content/jobs/members_and_committees.php
- Presidential Management Fellows (PMF) Program: Executive program that places fellows in a range of government agencies. http://www.pmf.gov/
- White House Fellows Program: Yearlong fellowship with White House staff members and other government officials. https://www.whitehouse.gov/about/fellows
- US Agency for International Development (USAID): Full-time positions and fellowships. http://www.usaid.gov/careers/
- US Department of Health and Human Services: Agency for Healthcare Policy and Research: https://www.ahrq.gov/cpi/about/careers/index.html
- US Department of Education: Positions in the Department of Education. http://www.ed.gov/jobs

- US Environmental Protection Agency: https://www.epa.gov/careers
- US Department of the Interior, Office of Environmental Policy: Office within the Interior department focused on environmental stewardship of natural resources http://www.doi.gov/jobs

Other Resources — Commercial sites

- Federal Government Jobs: Opportunities in federal government and resource materials. http://www.federaljobs.net/
- Gov't Jobs: Aggregation of local, state, and federal level government jobs. http://www.govtjobs.com/
- Federal government jobs and job search services. https://www.federaljobsearch.com
- US Department of Defense civilian jobs: http://godefense.cpms.osd.mil/employment.aspx

State and Local Government

- Each state and city government will have its own websites for open positions—remember that every state and many cities will have agencies that mirror the federal agencies.
- GovtJob.Net: Job opportunities in local governments across the country. http://www.govtjob.net/

Useful Job Boards for Selected Other Sectors

Arts and Culture

- Massachusetts Culture Jobs: Culturally focused jobs in the state of Massachusetts. https://www.hireculture.org/
- National Recreation and Park Association: National listings of positions in park, culture, and recreation positions. http://careercenter.nrpa.org/jobs
- Oregon Regional Cultural Council: Arts positions in the Northwest. http://www.racc.org/resources/jobs
- Philadelphia Cultural Alliance: Cultural positions in Philadelphia and the larger Northeast region. http://www.philaculture.org/jobbank

Consulting Careers

- Consulting Bench: Profiles of major firms and jobs in consulting. http://www.consultingbench.com/
- Consultant Board: Positions in consulting and resources for applying to consulting positions. http://www.consultantsboard.com/
- Consulting Crossing: A range of consulting positions across different fields. http://www.consultingcrossing.com/#

Economics and Education

- Econ-Jobs: Large database of economist jobs in academia, government and the private sector. http://www.econ-jobs.com/
- Micro Finance Job Gateway: Wide range of international and domestic jobs. http://www.microfinancegateway.org/jobs-internships
- The Association for Education Finance and Policy: Positions in education policy research and education finance. http://www.aefpweb.org/career
- National Education Association: Positions at national education policy group and affiliates. http://www.nea.org/home/825.htm

Energy and the Environment

- American Council for an Energy Efficient Economy: Jobs with ACEEE and other energy policy groups. http://aceee.org/about/jobs
- Energy Central: Energy sector jobs. http://jobs.energycentral.com/
- Energy Crossing: Energy related jobs http://www.energycrossing.com/#
- Energy Jobs: Energy related jobs. http://www.energyjobs.com/
- Natural Resources Defense Council: National organization centered on environmental protection programs with a wide range of environmental policy positions. https://www.nrdc.org/careers
- Earthshare: Volunteer opportunities. http://www.earthshare.org/
- Environmental Career: http://www.environmentalcareer.com/
- Environmental Career Opportunities: http://www.ecojobs.com/
- Environmental Defense Fund: http://www.edf.org/jobs
- Greenbiz.com: http://jobs.greenbiz.com/
- Green Job Search: http://greenjobsearch.org/
- Green Jobs: Jobs in the field of renewable energy. http://www.greenjobs.com/

Health and Science Related

- AcademyHealth:. http://jobs.academyhealth.org
- Health Jobs USA: Healthcare jobs. http://www.healthjobsnationwide.com/
- BioCareers: Information about careers in science policy and the life sciences. http://biocareers.com/job-seekers
- Labratjobs: scientific research and science policy. http://www.thelabrat.com/
- SciDev Net: International jobs in science policy and development areas. http://www.scidev.net/global/content/jobs.html

Human Service and Social Work

- Alliance for Strong Families http://www.alliance1.org/solutions/job-board
- The Social Work Career Center https://www.socialworkers.org/joblinks/
- Social Work Job Bank: http://www.socialworkjobbank.com/site/

Planning and Urban Affairs

- American Planning Association: urban planning, transportation, urban policy. https://www.planning.org/jobs/
- The Urban Institute Job Board: Positions at the Urban Institute. http://www.urban.org/about/careers/
- Unionjobs.com: Positions at a variety of unions; search by position or location. http://www.unionjobs.com/

International Development and Aid, Global Organizations

- International Organization Careers (US Citizens): State Department's job board for positions in the UN and other international organizations. http://iocareers.state.gov/Main/Home
- World Bank: http://www.worldbank.org/
- DevNetJOBS: http://www.devnetjobs.org/
- Foreign Affairs: Positions at international NGOs, nonprofits, and governmental agencies. http://jobs.foreignaffairs.com/
- Global health http://globalhealth.org/resources/job-board/
- Development Aid: https://www.developmentaid.org/#!/jobs/search
- Expatriate Network: https://www.expatnetwork.com/
- Global Corps Job Listings: Positions at governmental international aid organizations. http://globalcorps.com/
- International Jobs Center: International jobs in a number of different fields. http://www.internationaljobs.org/hotjobs.html

Human Rights Groups

- Human Rights Watch: Positions in human rights advocacy. http://www.hrw.org/en/about/jobs
- Human Rights First: Positions in human rights advocacy. http://www.humanrightsfirst.org/careers

United Nations and related sites

- United Nations. http://www.un.org/en/index.html
- UNICEF: UN body organized to protect and advance the rights of children. http://www.unicef.org/about/employ/
- UNDP: United Nations Development Programme: UN body organized to provide financial and organizational assistance to developing nations. http://jobs.undp.org/
- UNJobs.org: UN and international NGO job opportunities. http://www.unjobs.org/

RF | Key Skill Sets

This **Resource File** offers some language describing the main four skill sets that employers seek in entry level and junior staff applicants.

Read these action phrases in the context of your own work experiences and *identify your own transferable skills. You can then use these phrases to build your resume bullets and develop your talking points.*

There are, of course, many other skills to master as you make your way professionally, but if you demonstrate that you have a few of the skills in each set, you can get a job and give yourself a chance to develop the rest.

Write your resume and craft your evolving narratives using resume bullets that include these action phrases (or similar phrases), which are *tied to your actual experiences in your internships, courses, jobs and extracurricular activities.*

For each position you seek, try to make sure that your resume bullets for these skills *use the same vocabulary and key words used in the job description's roles and responsibilities.*

1. Analytical And Problem Solving Skills

Description

- Visualizing, articulating, and solving both complex and uncomplicated problems and concepts; making decisions based on available information
- Applying logical thinking to gather and analyze information, design and test solutions to problems, and formulate plans
- Using logic and reasoning to identify the strengths and weaknesses of alternative solutions, conclusions or approaches to problems
- Developing capacities used to solve novel, ill-defined problems in complex, real-world settings

Transferable Skills — Quantitative

- Perform calculations
- Budget and forecast annual expenditures
- Compute, compare and organize quantitative data sets
- Research and analyze quantitative data sets using STATA/SPSS/SAS
- Conduct research in complex databases to acquire and analyze large datasets

Transferable Skills — Qualitative/General Research Skills/Problem Solving

- Conduct observations
- Design experimental protocols for a qualitative study
- Combine and integrate information from disparate sources
- Identify irregular results; interpret data validity
- Evaluate hypotheses and data critically
- Reach and defend independent conclusions
- Recognize meaningful problems and questions for research
- Identify themes in open-ended commentary
- Synthesize data; summarize findings
- Conceptualize areas for further research
- Monitor policies, law, regulations; assess potential impact on programs and populations
- Identify problems; devise solutions
- Provide technical support
- Conduct program evaluations

2. Written and Verbal Communication Skills

Description

- Communicating effectively in writing as appropriate for the needs of the audience
- Effectively conveying information to others in conversation, in public presentations, and through appropriate channels of social media
- Practicing active listening, by giving full attention to what other people are saying; taking time to understand key points; not interrupting; asking questions as appropriate
- Persuading others to change their minds or behavior
- Negotiating to bring others together to reconcile difference and reach a solution

Transferable Skills

- Present research findings via written reports
- Synthesize and communicate results through graphical representations
- Proofread, edit, and/or write briefs, memos
- Author reports identifying problems and recommending initiatives
- Negotiate with internal and external stakeholders
- Translate memos, reports, briefs
- Deliver oral presentations in a clear and concise manner
- Articulate complex concepts to diverse constituents
- Advise clients/prospects
- Communicate project success criteria
- Persuasively support a position or viewpoint with argumentation and logic
- Write grant proposals
- Confirm and communicate client expectations
- Draft promotional/marketing materials
- Provide feedback
- Lobby
- Represent organizations to external audiences

3. Project Management Skills

Description

- Planning, organizing, securing, managing, leading, and controlling resources to achieve specific goals according to strict deadlines and budget
- Coordinating efforts of team members and third-party contractors or consultants to deliver projects and bring about beneficial change or added value

Transferable Skills — Planning and Execution

- Define project scope, goals, objectives and deliverables
- Direct, manage and strategize
- Develop full scale project plans and associated communications documents
- Plan and schedule project timelines and milestones using appropriate tools
- Develop and deliver progress reports, proposals, and presentations
- Proactively manage changes in project scope; construct project design and logistics
- Identify potential crises and devise contingency plans

- Evaluate program effectiveness by conducting project post mortems and creating recommendations report to identify successful and unsuccessful project elements
- Develop best practices and tools for project execution and management
- Identify and implement best practices
- Devise process designs and project plans
- Plan and implement large-scale events
- Independently initiate new projects
- Balance multiple projects under tight deadlines

Transferable Skills — Resource and Time Management

- Execute quality control mechanisms
- Estimate resources and staff and/or consultants needed to achieve project goals
- Draft and submit budget proposals
- Recommend subsequent budget changes

Transferable Skills — Coordination

- Participate in ongoing meetings with partner organizations to develop and execute proposals to support new experimental studies and ongoing research work
- Collaborate with senior management and stakeholders
- Communicate project expectations to team members and stakeholders
- Liaise with project stakeholders on an ongoing basis
- Set and manage project goals and objectives with colleagues
- Delegate tasks and responsibilities to appropriate personnel
- Build, develop and grow business relationships vital to the project's success
- Supervise team members
- Coordinate campaign logistics

4. Interpersonal and Leadership Skills

Description

- Monitor and assess your performance and others' to make improvements or take corrective action
- Motivate, develop and direct people as they work
- Identify the best people for the job
- Actively seek out opportunities to help people achieve their goals

- Maintain awareness of others' reactions and understand that individuals may react differently from one another
- Cultivate enhanced perception of non-verbal communication cues
- Strengthen leadership qualities such as integrity, dedication, magnanimity, openness, creativity, and fairness
- Develop positive assertive behaviors, such as:
  - Openness in expressing wishes, thoughts and feelings and encouraging others to do likewise
  - Listening to the views of others and responding appropriately, whether in agreement with these views or not
  - Accepting responsibilities and being able to delegate to others
  - Regularly expressing appreciation of others for what they have done or are doing
  - Being able to admit to mistakes and apologize, maintaining self control; and behaving as an equal to others

Transferable Skills
- Consult with internal and external stakeholders
- Lead team members
- Collaborate with cross divisional leadership
- Partner on internal initiative
- Mentor, coach, train
- Supervise project team members and vendor relationships
- Influence team members to take positive action and assume accountability for assigned work
- Brainstorm (and question) ideas in a group setting
- Monitor and assess personal performance
- Develop and maintain relationships with colleagues and clients
- Conduct outreach
- Engage in committee work; forge relationships with industry professionals
- Advise clients
- Develop and hone presentation skills
- Seek out opportunities for public speaking

RF | Advice for International Students

This **Resource File** focuses on some of the special challenges facing international students who are studying in the U.S. and hope to find a job for after they graduate.

Perhaps the most significant obstacle facing international students is simply a lack of knowledge about the range of possible available positions—which is the same obstacle faced by domestic students.

The solution? International students need to overcome any hesitations and **spend as much time in the career services office/library as possible.**

You need to meet with the career counselors early and often, and ask a lot of questions. Do not be shy. Be prepared with questions and if it takes more than one session with a counselor to get the answers, that's fine. **But don't expect the counselors to tell you what to do.** Your counselor is a resource to help you think about the information you need to discover, not an answer machine. *Only you can do the research, reading and networking that will lead you to a challenging job.*

Another key obstacle facing international (and domestic!) students can be a fear of risk taking. Learning to take social risks is hard, but it is a vital part of maturing as a young professional. Take small steps every day to increase your social confidence. Take a public speaking class, practice small talk with strangers, smile at people as you walk along. As you gain social confidence, you will project more and more competence, which will increase your chances of being hired.

Employment Challenges Facing International Students

There are many challenges facing international students who want to work in the U.S. during and after their study programs. I urge you to review the excellent book by Marcelo Barrios, *The International Advantage: Get Noticed. Get Hired.*

Some challenges relate to the employers

- Employers may hesitate to consider international students as candidates because they are either unfamiliar with, or misunderstand, the prevailing employment regulations. Indeed, the employment rules regarding international applicants may change, however there will always be some opportunities for non-U.S. citizens to work in the U.S.
- Unfortunately, the burden of knowing and being able to effectively communicate the current regulations often falls on the applicant, and this can be a real barrier if the employer will not take the time to master the regulations.
  - Many career services office have developed materials which you can share with potential employers—such as FAQ or Factsheets on Hiring International Students. Check with your career counselor!

Other challenges relate to the applicants themselves

- Many international students have unrealistic expectations about their job prospects in the U.S. It is important to realize that, under normal conditions, international students do not get special consideration for on-campus jobs or internships, and they must compete with domestic students who may have better soft skills or other relevant preparation.
- Students may come to the U.S. with the expectation that it will be relatively easy to find work that will enable them to stay in the U.S. after they graduate. Unfortunately, it is often much harder than expected to find an appropriate opportunity. Many students are disappointed, and then they lose hope that they will find a job in the U.S. and **they stop networking.**

It's important to keep networking even if it feels frustrating.

When you reach out to talk with people, be prepared to talk about what you have been doing to actively expand your network. How can you **demonstrate that you are a pro-active person** to someone meeting you for an information interview?

- **Do your homework and ask a good, targeted question.** For example, don't ask someone "how did you get to where you are today" but ask instead "I see you worked at company XYZ early in your career—can you share with me how that experience has informed the work you are doing now at company ABC" or "what were key lessons you learned from that early experience which have stayed with you in your career?"
- **Share relevant information about your other outreach activities.** For example, you can mention that you have been to a particular conference or that you volunteered on a project that they may find of interest.

■ **Show interest in their activities** and offer to help people with their projects. Mention ways you might to contribute to their efforts. You never know what might happen when you open up this way with someone.

Home Court Advantages

Each one of us has natural advantages and disadvantages when it comes to our careers. When you are living in your own country/city/community, you have a *home court advantage* over someone who is coming into your world. It's important to regularly take stock of your home court advantages, since they can point you to potential opportunities.

Some advantages include:
■ having native language proficiency,
■ having a place to live for free,
■ knowing people who will help you,
■ having the support of friends and family nearby.

International students who are studying outside of their home country should reflect carefully on how the skills and habits of mind that they are developing in the U.S. can help them succeed in their home environments, where they should also have some home court advantages.

Of course, not all American ways of doing things are culturally relevant outside the U.S., and it's important to be appropriately mindful of when and where to use American approaches to working, networking, and balancing life and work.

Self Promotion: It's Not Only For Americans

Many international students approach the job hunt at a social disadvantage when compared to some U.S. students because they are not culturally inclined to "sell themselves." Since no one is born knowing how to effectively promote themselves, everyone has to learn this critical skill. International students who come from cultural backgrounds that may disapprove of self-promotion can succeed in the U.S. market when they overcome their initial hesitation and find authentic ways to present themselves credibly to potential employers.

What are steps you can take to improve your self promotion skills?

■ **Practice introducing yourself.** Use your phone or video camera to tape yourself so you can see where you have challenges. Practice a lot!

■ **Practice shaking hands.** Americans value forthright, confident approaches to introducing yourself, so be sure to practice how to give a firm handshake while at the same time looking the person in the eye, smiling and saying "Hello, Mr. Smith" or whatever is appropriate at the moment.

■ **Work on near fluency in spoken English.** U.S. employers are highly unlikely to hire people who cannot easily communicate orally with their colleagues and supervisors. As an international student studying in the U.S. it is very important to maximize your opportunities to speak English, both formally in class and more informally with friends. If you spend all your time outside of class with friends from your home country, speaking your native language, you will sabotage yourself when it comes time to look for a work opportunity here.

■ **Sign up for the counseling and mock interview sessions** at your college career services office. Practice your explanation of who you are and what you are looking for, and practice making small talk. For example, make sure you know something about the local professional and college sports teams—especially if they are big winners. It is good to know the names of a few key players, and if a team is in town/has a game coming up.

How to Use Semester Breaks

There is an obvious dilemma facing international students studying in the U.S. when it comes to deciding how best to spend their time between semesters. With the hope of achieving their objective of working in the U.S. after graduation, many students appropriately seek out internships in the U.S. during summer breaks. But they do so at the *risk of failing to form meaningful employment connections in their home markets.* Since the vast majority of all international students return to their home countries after they finish studying abroad, it is in fact a risky decision to stay in the U.S. for the summer.

One possible strategy is to try to work at home in the summers and in the U.S. during the school year, though for many students it is not possible to travel home that often, and if you work in the U.S. *while you are still a student* you will impact your ability to work in the U.S. *after* you graduate (see CPT/OPT discussion, below.)

Try to be intentional about your potential options and create opportunities for yourself: if you can, *build your home country support network at the same time as you reach out for connections in the U.S.* Your classmates, both American and non-American, will be important resources for you; be sure you remember to return the favor and help them as much as they help you.

Think About Graduate School As Early as You Can

If you know you want to stay in the U.S. after you finish your undergraduate program, consider applying to graduate schools at the same time as you are seeking employment. If you are accepted to a graduate program, you can usually defer enrollment if you get a job offer that will qualify for OPT visa authorization.

Work Authorization Options

Be sure to check with your career services office and/or an attorney as these regulations are subject to change.

The **Curricular Practical Training (CPT)** Program covers F-1 students seeking work or internship related to their field of study during coursework. CPT participants may work either part-time (usually during the school year) or full-time (usually during the summer). Note that *after 12 months of full-time CPT, the student will not be eligible for OPT*—so this is an important factor to consider as you think about work options during semester breaks.

The **Optional Practical Training (OPT)** Program covers F-1 students pursuing part- or fulltime work, paid or unpaid, related to the field of study for 12 months immediately after the end of their program.

The **STEM Extension for OPT** applies to F-1 students in certain STEM (science, technology, engineering, mathematics) fields; students can receive a 24-month extension of the 12-month OPT, for a total of 36 months.

Academic Training (AT) Programs apply to J-1 students working or interning in positions related to their fields of study. AT programs apply during or immediately after program completion. The length of AT depends on the length of the program of study. During coursework, students can work less than 20 hours a week, but following end of coursework, students must work at least 20 hours a week.

H1-B visas are temporary, three-year work authorization permits for employees with employer sponsorship. They are renewable for three additional years. There is an annual quota on H1-B visas; however, employees of some organizations such as nonprofits, and research and educational institutions are exempt.

Original Source: University of California, Berkeley

RF | Applying to Graduate School

This **Resource File** offers some ideas about why and when you might want to consider earning a graduate degree—and what sort of graduate degree to pursue.

The goal of this **Resource File** is to help you think about:
- Credential sequencing,
- Academic and professional graduate degree programs, and
- Graduate school application best practices.

It also offers suggestions for ensuring that you are a strong applicant if and when you decide to earn a graduate degree. Be sure to review the discussion of the opportunity costs and benefits of pursuing additional training in **Chapter Three.**

Why and When to Undertake Graduate Study

For most college graduates, the prospect of *immediately* continuing their education past the Bachelor's Degree is both undesirable and unreasonable. While there are some students who go directly to graduate school after finishing college, they are a minority of the graduate student population, since *many graduate programs require applicants to have one, two or more years of post-college work experience.*

Additionally, most students need a break from school and some experience working in the real world—if only to earn some money so that they can support themselves and take the steps necessary to establish themselves as independent adults.

International students currently earning Bachelor's Degrees may want to apply to graduate programs as a *back up* plan in case they do not find employment that will enable them to stay in the U.S. after graduation. ***Although some graduate programs require work experience, there are many others that do not.*** Creating graduate school options for yourself will take some effort, and you may decide you prefer to return home rather than go directly to a graduate program, however it can be empowering to create some study options for yourself, even if you don't end up enrolling.

As you move forward in your career, you will need to constantly revisit the question of your own credentials and training. Are your skills and degrees sufficient for the job(s) that you see yourself in 3, 5 or 10 years in the future? If not, how can you gain the skills you need while still working full time? Alternatively, should you consider—and can you afford—taking a break from working full time to focus on a graduate program?

Many people turn to graduate programs after they have spent two or three years working at an entry level position. They identify the next position they want and see that to be competitive, they are going to need another degree.

Or they decide that they want to pivot in their career trajectory and focus their attention on a new subject/enter a new field—and they will use graduate school as their platform to launch that new career.

While in the past it was fairly uncommon to pursue multiple graduate degrees over the course of a career, it is now much more likely that young professionals will find that—at some point in their careers—they will need to pursue additional training and/or graduate study toward a degree.

Graduate Degrees—What Standardized Exam to Take?

The most common graduate education degree programs are Master's and Doctoral degrees. You can earn a Master of Arts (M.A.) or Master of Science (M.S.) or Doctor of Philosophy (Ph.D.) degree in many different subjects. You can even become a doctor or a lawyer in the U.S. despite not having studied those subjects as an undergraduate. In the U.S., people who wish to be lawyers or doctors first complete their Bachelor's degree (in any subject) and then enroll in either a Juris Doctor (J.D.) or Medical Doctor (M.D.) program.

- To be admitted to most masters and doctorate graduate programs in the arts and sciences, you will need to take a standardized test called the Graduate Record Exam (GRE)
- To be admitted to most graduate business programs, you will need to take the Graduate Management Admission Test (GMAT), though there are some schools that accept a GRE score instead of the GMAT.
- To be admitted to medical school you will need to take the Medical College Admission Test (MCAT) and you may need to take some science courses if you did not take them in college.

- To be admitted to law school you will need to take the Law School Admissions Test (LSAT), though there are some schools that accept the GRE instead of the LSAT, or which do not require a standardized test score at all.
  - If you already have an undergraduate degree in law from another country, you may elect to enroll in a Master's in Law program (LL.M), and in this case you will not need the LSAT score.

Graduate Degrees—terminal, academic, professional

In the Unites States, graduate degree programs may be characterized as either "terminal" or not, and as either "academic" or "professional." The distinctions between these categories are related to the academic achievement needed in order to practice a specific profession or to pursue a career as a professor at the college/university level.

- **Terminal Degrees:** By definition, a terminal degree can be either the highest possible academic attainment in a subject, or it can be awarded when a person completes a fixed amount of graduate work but elects not to continue to earn the PhD. Hence, there are terminal Master's degree programs, which signal sufficient mastery of a subject for professional practice, yet students may also use such a terminal Master's program to prepare for a Ph.D. program.
- **Academic Degrees:** For most academic fields, the highest degree that can be earned is a Ph.D. in that subject. Those who want to be eligible for tenured/tenure track positions in a college or university need to earn their Ph.D. in the subject they wish to teach. The traditional exception is law, as law professors can teach and be tenured with a J.D., which is the same terminal, professional degree that practicing lawyers earn. The word terminal is not used very much outside the United States, and in fact, there are some graduate degrees which are even higher than Ph.D.s, such as the *habilitation* degree in Germany.
- **Professional degrees:** These have historically been degrees that, either by law or custom, have been required for certain professions. Familiar examples include the degrees for lawyers and doctors: Juris Doctor (J.D.) and Doctor of Medicine (M.D.) respectively. There are a few other widely recognized professions that expect students to earn a specific undergraduate or graduate degree representing an approved course of study, including accounting, business, design, engineering, and healthcare.

More and more management positions require some data analytics familiarity, so as people seek out more challenges and more responsibility, they are increasingly taking the opportunity to earn Master's degrees that offer them these technical skills along with substantive, specialized knowledge in their field of interest.

There Are Many New Master's Degree Programs

There has been significant proliferation of different kinds of Master's degree programs as colleges and universities have responded to the demand in the market for more specialized professionals—and as the nature of professional work has shifted in response to society's rapid digital transformation. There are now as many different Master's degree programs as colleges can think up—with more being developed every day, including some that are offered partially or completely online.

These newer graduate degrees are generally either M.A. (Master of Arts) or M.S. (Master of Sciences) degrees *in a particular subject*.

For just one example out of many possible schools to focus on, the University of Colorado at Denver offers *over 100 different graduate Master's degrees:*
- http://www.ucdenver.edu/programs/masters/Pages/default.aspx

The M.S. and M.A. degrees can be offered for many different subjects and different concentrations or tracks within a subject. At CU Denver, there are 4 different tracks for an M.S. in Accounting; and 4 different tracks for an M.A. in Anthropology!

There are also other Master's degrees with different initials corresponding to their fields, such as:
- M.B.A. Master of Business Administration
- M.P.A. Master of Public Administration
- M.P.P. Master of Public Policy
- M.C.J. Master of Criminal Justice
- M. Eng Master of Engineering
- LL.M. Master of Laws (requires a prior first degree in law)

Every university offers a different roster of degree programs, and although the requirements for admission will be similar at most major universities, they will vary enough that you need to do careful research on the particular program(s) that interest you.

Doctoral Graduate Degree Programs Are Still Popular

As noted above, graduate degree programs leading to the Ph.D. in a particular subject area (eg Ph.D .in Math, Biology, Psychology, English, Comparative Literature, etc) are designed to train the next generation of faculty who will teach and do research at the college/university level.

These programs may offer students a Master's degree that is earned midway through the doctoral program, (M.A. for the Arts/Humanities and M.S. for the Sciences), and some students may drop out of doctoral programs either "ABD" ("all but the dissertation") or when they earn the Master's degree.

Traditionally, students who did not finish their Ph.D.'s did not usually go on to teach the subject at university level, but instead found work in other areas—perhaps related to their subject area, but not always. Teaching at the primary or secondary level (high school) is always a possibility without a Ph.D., and specialized journals might hire MA/MS or ABD graduates to work as editors, or private companies might hire them to help with technical writing or product development and operations management. Students in the STEM fields who earn Ph.D.s will either pursue teaching jobs, or continue their research as "post Docs" in academic or corporate settings.

Of course the opportunities available to graduates of different disciplines are diverse, however in general, the point is that without the "earned Ph.D." it was (and still is) very difficult to be hired as a full time faculty member at a college or university.

Colleges and universities are shifting toward a more contingent workforce, which means going forward they will hire fewer tenured faculty and more part time, adjunct teachers. For a range of subjects, they are also increasingly hiring practitioners who may only hold Master's degrees but are considered qualified to teach based on their years of experience in the real world. However, and especially for teaching doctrinal courses in most fields of study, an earned Ph.D. will likely remain the prerequisite for an academic appointment, whether tenure track or not.

Adjuncts are hired by the course and many have to teach at more than one school to earn enough to support themselves teaching. On the one hand, this means that many more people are getting the chance to teach at the university level than in the past; on the other hand, these adjuncts are doing so under very difficult conditions and without the protections and benefits of full time employment such as paid vacation, sick leave, and support for continued research and professional development. Most adjuncts have earned Ph.D's in their fields, but have not been able to secure a full time position because of the changes taking place in the colleges and universities.

Why do people continue to enroll in Ph.D. programs if the employment and teaching prospects are not as good as they used to be?

There are many reasons, including:

- The subject area of the Ph.D. is incredibly interesting to the student,
- Being admitted to a Ph.D. program usually means that you are awarded financial aid to cover tuition and living expenses while you study,
- Teaching at any level can be emotionally and professionally rewarding, and
- Having a Ph.D. is prestigious, and even if you don't become a university professor, many companies and organizations look to hire people with Ph.D's.

So while earning a Ph.D. will no longer necessarily set you up for a university teaching career, it is usually a wonderful intellectual and personal experience, and there are an increasing number of professional career paths that newly-minted Ph.D's can explore. The Chronicle of Higher Education (www.chronicle.com) is an invaluable resource for anyone thinking of earning a Ph.D. and/or about a career in academia—be sure to spend time on the site and reach out to faculty in the field for advice.

How to pick a U.S. Graduate School program

Once you have decided to think about furthering your education with enrollment in a graduate program, you face the challenge of figuring out what to study and where to go to get that education.

If you are already studying in the United States, you may wish to continue on directly to graduate school, however be aware that many programs require applicants to have work experience—usually 2–3 years—after completion of their undergraduate degrees. So you will need to find employment either in the US or elsewhere, and then apply to the schools you are considering sometime in the second or third year after finishing your B.A. degree.

If you are still on campus, you can start doing research on possible graduate programs by first checking out the resources available to you. The career services office will have a library of resource books and materials that you can read to learn about different graduate programs, and your professors and career counselors can also help you explore your ideas and suggest possible programs. Even if you have graduated and are working, you still have access to these resources. You can also review similar materials in the public library, at a local bookstore or online.

There are 50 States in the U.S. and every single one of them has one or more universities, and numerous colleges offering a wide range of instruction. For our purposes, we will assume that you only want to attend an accredited, well regarded program at a university that meets your other criteria such as location, reputation, program rigor, price and level of competition for admission.

Here are some Graduate School application resources you may wish to consider:
- http://pitweb.pitzer.edu/career-services/students/graduate-school/
- http://idealistgradschool.org/learn-about-grad-school/
- http://poetsandquants.com/specialized-masters/

An invaluable resource is the U.S. News and World Report Rankings, which are issued annually and can be seen here:
- http://grad-schools.usnews.rankingsandreviews.com/best-graduate-schools

However, the "best" schools as ranked by U.S. News may not be the best ones for you.

Here are some other factors to consider as you begin to think about where you want to attend graduate school:
- By subject/specialty and faculty and then by Rank of the University — or vice versa
- By Location and then Subject/Specialty and faculty and then University Rank
- By recommendations from Professors, Friends and Family
- By employer payment options
- By price

Price: You will need to spend time on the websites of the programs you are considering to find out the particular details of each school's tuition, scholarship and financial aid policies.

Price is an important consideration because if you need to borrow money to attend graduate school, the more you owe upon graduation, the more pressure there will be for you to quickly secure a high paying job — in whatever field/for whatever company you can find, and not necessarily the one you have just earned your degree in!

The top schools' programs are very expensive and many professional programs (those that do not lead to Ph.D's) do not offer scholarships or financial aid. Of course there are some professional programs, including those at the top schools, which DO offer scholarships and financial aid (for example a tuition reduction associated with a teaching assistantship.)

Fit: Another aspect to choosing your graduate program is "fit"—this means that the program offers what you are interested in and faculty who teach and research in the areas that interest you, that your qualifications meet or exceed their admissions requirements, and that your academic learning style and personality match the behavioral and professional expectations of that program's faculty and students.

Location and weather are also important considerations, because if you are someone who hates big cities, then an urban graduate program won't make you happy, and if you get bored easily/like a lot of diverse distractions, then you will not be happy on a campus that is too far away from a city to go out on a Friday night! And of course if you really hate cold weather and snow and all the things that go along with winter, then you won't want to choose a program—no matter how great it seems otherwise—that is in one of the more northern states such as Maine, Minnesota or North Dakota.

If at all possible, you should try to visit the schools that you are considering so that you can walk around and get a feel for the place. While of course you are an applicant, you are also a consumer and you will find that there is a lot of benefit to putting a strong effort into your research and investigation of potential programs. Then, after you have applied and (hopefully) been accepted to a few, you can compare their offers and make an informed decision about where you want to study.

Notice that I am suggesting that you apply to more than one school: this is because, obviously, you may not be accepted to your #1 choice program, or you may be accepted but not offered sufficient financial aid by that school. If you have competing admissions offers, and one school offers partial or even full tuition remission but the other does not, you will need to carefully consider your options and seek out advice.

In addition to the general *opportunity cost analysis* factors cited in **Chapter Three,** consider these points:
- highly ranked schools tend to offer less scholarship money than lower ranked schools,
- highly ranked business schools often require candidates to have several years of work experience,
- program rank may be only loosely correlated with the earning power of the credential,
- programs tend to have strong alumni networks in certain cities, so it matters where you want to live after graduate school,

- Ph.D. programs in particular subjects and at particular schools may account for the majority of the faculty who get tenure track appointments,
- your personal cost of living may vary significantly as between programs, so its important to take into account your true costs.

If you are not 100% sure about pursuing an academic career, but you really want to pursue a graduate degree, be sure to take some time to think about possible career options after you complete the degree. A good place to start is at this website: http://www.phds.org/jobs. This very up-to-date site has also aggregated a lot of excellent advice for applicants to graduate programs of all types.

Another excellent resource to consider as you think about graduate study is this site: http://www.mastersindatascience.org/ where you will find an aggregation of resources associated with studying and pursuing a career in data science and analytics.

Preparing for Graduate School while in College

How can you prepare yourself to be a competitive graduate school applicant if you have no idea when—or even if—you want to go to graduate school? The most successful college students know that it is in their interest to work at internships and other part time jobs while they are in college so that they can:

- start to create a network of references who can speak to their work habits,
- learn important work related skills that are not taught in college, and
- experience the projects and assignments that different jobs require.

These *strategies for preparing to enter the workforce do not conflict with the strategies needed to make you a strong competitive applicant for graduate school*—they can and should complement your ongoing academic efforts.

Even as you prepare yourself to enter the workforce after you graduate, while you are still in college, it is prudent to do the following:

- **Take the opportunity to get to know one or more professors who can serve as references for you in the future.**

Your goal is to be able to show that you are a strong student, both in terms of your grades and as evidence of your capacity to do more advanced research. Graduate school admissions teams are looking for candidates whose college transcripts demonstrate their *academic abilities*—that is, their potential to do original research and contribute to the development of new ideas and new approaches to the subject. References from one or more of your professors are a vital component of your graduate school application and *professional references from your supervisors at work do not substitute for academic references.*

Do not panic if you are applying to graduate school a few years after you graduated. If you cannot obtain any academic references from college professors, you can take a refresher course at a community college—maybe a statistics course?—and get to know that professor. This is also a good strategy for demonstrating that you can do well academically, which can help improve an older, less-than-stellar college transcript.

However, if you can, it is a good idea to try to reach out to one or more of your old professors and ask for their help. Send an email explaining who you are ("I took your Intro to Psych class in Fall 2014") and why you are writing now. Explain that

- you are applying to graduate program(s) at ABC and XYZ schools and the deadline for reference submissions is January 1, 2019,
- you are interested in these programs because…describe specific faculty research or other details about the programs and how they relate to your interests now, and
- you have been working for the past 3 years since graduating in a series of jobs, learning about whatever you have learned about, and now you realize you want to do a graduate degree in whatever it is you want to study—try to link what you have learned with what you want to study if there is a link—even if it is just to say that you changed your mind about what you are interested in as a result of doing this work over the past few years.

Familiarize yourself with the different kinds of graduate degrees that relate in some way to your interests.

- Your career services office will have materials that you can read—put aside an hour or two and take the time to read about different graduate programs and the careers they can support. Or search online and read what different programs say about their degrees and the kinds of jobs that their students take when they graduate.

Look at the professional profiles of people who are working in jobs that you are interested in — what degrees and certificates do those people have?

- If you get the opportunity to do an informational interview with one of those people, ask about their graduate program. What did they like about the school they attended? What advice would they offer to you if you were looking at graduate programs? File away their advice for the future, and be sure to circle back to them if you do decide to apply to their ***alma mater.*** [Latin phrase commonly used for the school or university a person has attended.]

Applying to Graduate Programs

Every graduate program is a little different in terms of what the admissions office is looking for from strong applicants, however several common attributes of successful applications are:

- Competitive standardized test scores. Competitive scores will be in the top end of the range accepted by that school; also note that all programs consider test scores as part of a holistic evaluation of the applicant.
- A strong narrative (personal statement) that:
  - Demonstrates superior writing ability.
  - Offers a coherent argument for why the applicant is a good candidate for the program.
  - Shows the applicant's *Emotional Intelligence* in addition to their academic qualifications. Graduate programs are looking for people who are mature and self-aware.
- Several strong academic and professional references.
- Clear evidence of prior academic achievement, including progressive improvement in grades if necessary. If your academic performance as an undergraduate was not stellar, that does not mean you will not be admitted to the graduate program of your choice, but it does mean that you need to have a strategy for explaining your grades and demonstrating your potential to succeed in an academic environment now.
- For Ph.D. programs, a clear explanation of how your proposed research complements the research interests of one or more of the current faculty.

Writing A Winning Personal Statement

How can you make sure that your personal statement makes a compelling case to the reader that you are a good candidate for the program? Here are some basic guidelines for drafting your personal statement:

Do's

- Open strong with attention grabbing, theme setting sentences
- Write in your own voice
- Refer to the school's programs or particular professors as they relate to your scholarly/academic/professional interests
- Explain your professional goals and how your trajectory toward those goals will be supported by this specific graduate program
- Demonstrate your mastery of English—and English grammar
- Use proper syntax and understand the meaning of all your words
- Use effective transition sentences for new paragraphs
- Follow any page or word limits and if sending printed documents, make sure these are neatly typed with your name on each page
- Close strong and refer back to your opening theme
- Have a friend review your statement—another pair of eyes can help make it stronger and also help avoid spelling, grammar or other mistakes

Don'ts

- Forget to change the name of the school in the statement if applying to many schools with the same essay
- Use the passive voice or repeat yourself
- Use clichés or offer excuses for anomalies—only clear explanations
- Simply restate your resume
- Rely on the computer spell check program

Additional notes on applying to Academic Ph.D. Programs

Applicants admitted to Ph.D. programs can usually expect a package of financial support that includes tuition and some amount of stipend or fellowship to help cover living expenses. Financial packages will usually include financial support for several years of study—perhaps as few as 3 years or as many as 6 years, depending on the strength of the school, the program and the candidate.

The way that most academically oriented Ph.D. graduate programs admit students is as follows:

- The admissions team will review the application to make sure it meets the minimum requirements of the program and is a complete file including all references, transcripts, and other required components.
- Depending on the school, the admissions team may provide a preliminary review of the application on the merits, but in most programs, the Ph.D. candidate files are reviewed and ranked by a committee of the faculty. These professors are best able to assess the credentials—and especially the academic references—that are submitted to them.
- The faculty are looking to admit a group of incoming doctoral candidates whose research interests will match or complement the work that already enrolled students are doing as well as relate in some significant way to their own specialties.
- Every program is different and from one year to the next, each year's recruitment expectations are different.
- The faculty committee will accept only the students they expect to enroll.

Since fitting in with the current research interests of the faculty is so important, if you decide to apply to a Ph.D. program, **one of the most important steps to take is to network your way to the faculty at that program who are doing the research that is closest to your interest.** There are multiple ways to approach this task, and the sooner you get started on it, the better, since you may find that connecting to the faculty at the program(s) where you want to apply will take some time.

For instance, you can start your research on which programs to apply to by reaching out to a college professor who works in the field that you wish to pursue. Ideally, you actually took a course with that professor so that they can also serve as an academic reference for you (if they are willing.)

If you are exploring a field for graduate work that is not related to what you studied as an undergraduate, don't despair. You can reach out to a professor at your college—you are now an alumnus so they should reply to your polite email asking for a few moments of their time. Email and ask them for their advice and if they would be willing to speak with you a few moments by phone, or, ideally, if you could meet with them at their convenience.

If you do not already know them well, consider this a request for an information interview and do your homework! Read about the professor's research and when you do speak with them, ask them for ideas, suggestions and referrals in regard to your proposed research project.

Take Aways from this Resource File

- **Think ahead.** You can prepare while still in college to be a competitive applicant for graduate school, and you can consult with college career services and faculty about graduate programs. Once you are out of college, plan ways to make yourself even more competitive to the graduate schools by taking statistics or an introductory doctrinal course.
- **Explore Your Options.** There are many different graduate programs, all looking for students. If you find a few that interest you and you can meet the admissions requirements, apply to more than one program.
- **Use Graduate Study to Grow and/or to Pivot in Your Career.** When you earn a graduate degree you are sending a message to the market that you are specialized in a particular subject area. Be sure to use the time in graduate school to strengthen your professional network by getting to know the other students in your cohort and learning how to tap into the program's alumni.

RF | Writing Style Guide

Dean Lazar's Golden Style Guide to Writing Well On the Job

I Introduction

The primary purpose of this style guide is to offer readers practical writing style suggestions and examples to use in different work related writing assignments. Format, style, tone and strategy are explained and the style guide includes examples of different letter and memo formats which can be used.

Your goal is to increase the clarity of your work-related communication. You should be able to write clear, concise written documents, and your written communication should be appropriate for each assignment. By following these guidelines, your writing will be more productive because clear, concise, better written documents will enable respondents to move quickly, identify what needs to be done, and act appropriately. Additionally, and critically, you will demonstrate to the people you work with—and report to—that you are an effective team player who can produce documents that stand alone and do not require a person hovering nearby to explain them to the reader.

This style guide will help you quickly adapt your writing style to the norms of your organization. When someone begins a new job, they often find that their written work is continually revised by others because the writer is unaware of the writing style required by the organization. By practicing clear expository writing from the outset, your work will require less basic revision by your managers, and you will be able to learn more easily what stylistic norms your organization requires from your writing.

One important *caveat* (warning): perhaps the most challenging thing to remember is that some work communications should NOT be written down—not in email, not in instant messaging apps, not in paper form. Think about your purpose in communicating and, if appropriate, consider picking up the phone or walking to someone's desk and speaking with them face-to-face.

II Strategies for Better Writing: Context and Purpose of the Document

1. Audience

The written documents we produce depend on the assignments we are given. There are many document formats in the business world, some of which you may use almost daily, and others you may never use at all. Individuals in different professions employ document formats unique to their line of work. You may be asked to develop documents to describe changes in policy and procedure, to communicate the findings and/or results of research or of new programs, or to request information from co-workers and supervisors.

Before you begin to write a memo, letter or report, you should ask yourself who will be reading the document, and what is the purpose of the communication. Written documents require different tones and styles depending on the intended reader. If you forget to think about these issues, your writing may not be as clear as it should be and the intended meaning may get lost. In the end, your objective may not be fulfilled—or worse, your words may be the cause of unintended consequences.

Because electronic communications such as email and social media have increased the speed and the reach of all our words, we must take special care to ensure that the words we put out there truly reflect our intentions and our best efforts. We must consider not only the intended reader, but any other possible other readers as well: before you hit send on your keyboard, you should re-read the document carefully and consider what might occur if its contents were to go viral/be made public.

As you begin to write the document, *think about the content and the specific information you are trying to convey*. Are you requesting some action from the intended reader, or are you just informing the reader about a change in policy? Are you making recommendations, which you want the reader to implement? Are you as the writer responding to a request or an event, or are you initiating the discussion of a specific issue?

The answers to these questions will help determine the format, tone and style of the document you are preparing. You must then decide on the format you will use to present the information, the tone you will use to get the reader's attention, and the style you will use to get the results you want.

2. Action Required by the Reader

Many of the written documents we prepare require some action by the intended reader. Working within large organizations often requires us to ask others for the information we need to do our jobs. We initiate or strengthen our working relationships through the written documents we distribute throughout the organization. In order to successfully get the information you need, you must be able to clearly define and communicate what you need, in writing, to the reader.

There are three important points to remember when requesting action from your reader.

- First, inform the reader at the beginning of the document that you are requesting action from him/her/them.
- Secondly, describe the purpose of your request and tell the reader exactly what information or action you desire. Be clear and concise: do not try and mask the fact that you need their assistance because they may miss the point and not respond.
- Lastly, try to provide the reader with all of the information they will need to fulfill your request. If the reader has any unanswered questions in their mind after reading the document they may not be able to do what you ask just from reading the document.

For example, if you need to request information about a work team's technical operations, you may want to use a memo format. The memo should be kept brief and, since you are requesting a response, the information you need should be presented as early as possible in the document, followed by a deadline you have set/requested for the response.

The tone should be semi-formal since you are requesting assistance/information, and you may want to use the active voice because it tends to be clear and more direct than the passive voice. [See below, Effective Tone, section V, for more on the distinction between the active and passive voice in English writing.]

3. Urgency of the Document

Because people tend to work on several projects simultaneously, your request for action or assistance may not have the same urgency to the reader as it does to you. The reader may take note of your request but forget to respond. Therefore, when preparing your document, you need to think about when you want the information or the action and the best way to ensure a prompt response.

There are two components to every deadline. First there is the deadline you have established for the reader to respond to your request. Second, there is the deadline established by your supervisor for completion of your project. Therefore, it is very important to keep your own deadline in mind before you set a deadline for those responding to your request.

How to establish a deadline for others

- Think about what you need to do with the information once you receive it and how much time that will take.
- If you need to analyze the data and prepare a brief report, establish a reasonable time frame for this activity. The deadline you set for the reader should take these activities into account and provide both you and others with adequate time for completion.
- Be sure to allow enough time between your own deadline and the reader's deadline in case the reader is unable to respond as quickly as you request.

It is important that the deadline be clearly and quickly defined in the document. If the reader cannot find the deadline, chances are they will not respond to it. Use bold lettering, capital letters, spacing or underlining to ensure that the deadline is readily visible. Do not bury the deadline in a long paragraph or at the end of the document.

Deadlines should include the following information:
- The day, date, and the time the information is to be submitted
- If there is actual physical material, where it is to be sent
- Who should be the primary recipient, and who is to be copied

The reader should be able to glance at the document and easily see the deadline without having to re-read the entire narrative.

4. Recommendations of the Writer

You may be asked to evaluate or research various products or programs and make recommendations from among the alternatives. These assignments are important because the implementation of your recommendations may have a significant impact on the organization. Such writing also is important because it demonstrates the quality of your thinking/analysis to your colleagues and supervisors. Finally, writing projects that require your own analysis are good writing samples for you to have in your portfolio, appropriately redacted as necessary to protect confidential information.

When analyzing various options and making recommendations, remember that you are trying to persuade the reader to take the action that you recommend. Your recommendations should result from comparing the similarities, differences, advantages and disadvantages of all the options you have considered. A complete analysis will include the strengths and drawbacks of several options because this factual information gives the analysis credibility and enables you to justify your recommendations.

Here is a basic outline for preparing recommendations based on an analysis of options. Whether in letter, memo or table/chart form, your goal is to present the analysis and the conclusions in a way which will make it easy for the reader to understand the rationale behind your recommendation.

- Briefly introduce the problem and the recommended action
- Provide a more detailed explanation of the problem
- Describe your analysis and explain the various options available for the solving the problem. Always remember to list the preferred options first, and for each one, discuss the advantages prior to the disadvantages
- Detail your recommendations and, if appropriate, identify the names of those individuals who could be tasked with implementing each recommendation.

III Strategies: How to Create Organized and Clear Documents

I assure you that the most useful strategy to develop a clearly written work product is to give yourself the time to do multiple drafts.

1. Writer's Block: Free Writing

Many of us develop special skills or have received technical training making us specialists in a particular discipline. You may become an engineer, a research or data analyst, a brand manager or marketing consultant or other kind of expert. No matter what the discipline, business writing is likely to be a significant part of your job. You will always communicate in writing about what you are doing.

Because you may not consider yourself a writer, you may sometimes find it hard to sit down and write the memos or reports required by your professional role. This is sometimes referred to as "writer's block"—you may find yourself sitting and staring at the screen, unable to begin writing.

Free writing is an effective way to get those initial thoughts flowing. The technique involves identifying the topic to be written about and taking a few minutes to think about what you want to write. Once you have a few thoughts in mind, begin writing them, without worrying about grammar, format, tone, style or spelling. Let your thoughts flow as if you were explaining them to someone sitting across from you. Write down subjects and phrases, using one word—or many— to capture the ideas. You may wish to use a piece of paper to do this, or to do it on a screen but then print the page out and use it as a checklist while writing the actual document.

Try to fill the page with your thoughts and ideas and remember, the more you think of now, the easier it will be to compose the document later because you'll be able to use this list of ideas to remind you of what to include.

The next step is to revise the freely written list of ideas into a memo, letter or other document.
- Start by going through the list and grouping your ideas.
  - Think about your priorities and decide which points belong together and the order in which they should appear in the document.
  - These numbered, grouped points will comprise your paragraphs.
- You should look at each set of points and try to write paragraphs for each set that incorporate all the important points.
  - The paragraphs can be moved around if the argument will make more sense in a different order.
- You may have to re-write the document several times, until your ideas have become clear and concise.
- **Do not throw away your original list with all the ideas and points until you have completed the final writing.** You will want to refer to (and even add to) this original source document as you are writing, and certainly be sure to double check as you finalize your document that you have not forgotten any important points that were early ideas.

You may think that free writing a list of ideas is a waste of time. However, this technique can be an effective tool for:
- Moving past writer's block
- Getting all your thoughts out and onto paper/screen—you may even come up with additional ideas you would not have thought of otherwise!
- Ensuring that you do not forget to include important points

2. Writer's Block: Mapping and Outlining

Another good technique which can help you conquer writer's block is to prepare a picture prior to writing the actual document. Sometimes referred to as mapping, this technique helps you organize your ideas and plan the document. Carefully planning a written document can help ensure you meet your objectives. It is especially good when you are writing a long document.

Mapping also begins with free writing—making a list of the ideas you want to include in the document. The next step is to group the ideas, by selecting the most important ideas, connecting the related ideas and prioritizing the ideas to tell the story you want to convey to your reader. The map you then develop from this prioritized list of grouped ideas can be arranged is a flow chart or not—but the basic idea is to arrange your grouped ideas/points on the page in a way that lets you visualize your argument. This map is a working document and you should feel free to use different colors, bold circles and thick or thin lines to connect related ideas and to separate broad themes from smaller details. There are many different examples of flowcharts on the Internet.

Outlining: You may also want to try to organize your ideas by preparing an outline. An outline can be the first thing you do, it can be the next step after mapping, or it can come directly from your list of ideas. There are a variety of outline formats you can use to organize your ideas, and the outline format you should choose depends on the document you need to prepare.

In general, an outline is a list of the headings that will comprise your document. For example, an introduction, several sections and perhaps subsections, and a conclusion.

You will then start to fill in the sections based on your map or your list of ideas.

In the introduction you will introduce the subject and explain the format of the remainder of the document. Depending on the length and complexity of the document, the introductory section can consist of a sentence, a paragraph, or even several paragraphs. It may be necessary to define some terminology or set the context of the document by providing a brief history of the topic. If the document is offering a recommendation, you will probably want to include that recommendation in the introductory paragraph—or you may create an Executive Summary section that precedes the introduction and provide your conclusions there.

After the introduction, you discuss the main points of the document. To help develop the main section(s), you should answer the following questions from the reader's point of view:

- What is the essential issue being discussed?
- What does the document ask the reader to do about the essential issue?
- What is the reader's interest in the issue?
- What are the short and long-term alternatives available to the reader?
- When and how are any proposals going to be implemented?

The next sections of your document will depend on your goals and the type of document you are preparing. After the discussion of the main point, alternatives, and related critical information, there may be additional information you need to convey. This information can be arranged in a variety of ways:

- *chronological order:* events written up in the order that they occurred, such as the itinerary in a trip report
- *decreasing order of importance:* this is often used in job descriptions or when presenting alternative solutions
- *persuasive order:* this is used when building an argument and justifying conclusions and recommendations
- *sequential order:* the stating of information in the order in which it should be carried out, such as instructions
- *comparison/contrast:* useful for describing similarities and differences, such as in an analysis of options.

Finally, a **Conclusion** section should close the main body of the document. The text in this section may be repeated at the start of the document in the Executive Summary. Any Supplemental data or Appendices follow the Conclusion.

3. Drafting and Revising

Once you have created an outline, you can begin writing the document. Drafting and rewriting the document should help make it clearer. For every revision, try to look at the document as if it is the first time you are reading it and pretend you know nothing about the subject. Most importantly, the document must be able to stand alone—that is, the writer should not have to accompany the document to explain it to the reader.

In addition to helping you create a clean, crisp final document, drafting has other purposes as well. Drafting allows you to write about the areas you are most comfortable with and leave the more difficult parts until later. If you are missing information, you can write around that part and develop a list of questions which you can work on at another time.

There are some techniques you can use to draft a document which will enable you to revise it easily. For example, when writing a draft, it can be helpful to use double spacing and begin every new section on a new page. Also, for long documents, as you work it may make sense to print out your outline and/or your draft pages to get the entire picture of the document in front of your eyes.

Drafting and revising will ultimately lead you to discard text that you feel is unnecessary. You may wish to save multiple versions of the document as you revise/delete, in case a detail you delete turns out to be important. You may find you are rethinking your objectives as you write and revise, and you always want to make sure that your writing strategy (and tone) suits your goals.

Rethinking your Strategy

At a certain point in the drafting/revising process, you may wish to ask yourself a series of key questions:

- Do I have a focus?
- Have I ordered the information in a way that makes it immediately clear to the reader?
- Have I thought of all my potential readers?
  - My manager
  - My manager's superiors
  - My colleagues
  - People who read the entire document
  - People who skim, browse or use it as a reference
- Have I left the reader knowing the answer to the question "So what?"
  - Is there focus and perspective?
  - Are there ideas for action?
  - Are there clear recommendations?

Editing and Reviewing

The next step when revising the document is to edit your text and any illustrations, tables or graphs you have included. Ask yourself if your writing "sounds right." Have you put the main ideas up front? Have you used action verbs? Does the document read well? (Try reading sentences out loud to see if they flow well together.) Make sure your illustrations, tables, and graphs make their points clearly.

The final phase of the revision process is to verify all of the information you have included in the document, ensure that your revisions are clear, and proof the document for spelling or grammar errors. Do not rely on the computer spellcheck! Try to look with an editor's eye at such details as headings and paragraph breaks, style, grammar and word choices, spelling and punctuation.

You should be sure to check your facts carefully and determine if your recommendations will be in compliance with your organization's policies and procedures. Or, if the recommendations imply or require changes in policy or procedures, you should be sure that you've made that clear to the reader.

If you can, have someone else do a quick review of the document before you submit it to your supervisor. It is often the case that someone who has never seen the material before will find errors you may have missed, or could offer you helpful editing suggestions. Of course due to timing, secrecy or other factors it may not be possible to have a second person review your work. If that is the case, at least try to give yourself enough time so you can let the final version sit for a day or so—and then you can give it a truly final review with your own fresh look.

4. Usefulness of Attachments/Hyperlinks

Attachments and/or hyperlinks to additional information can be used in any type of document to help illustrate the ideas presented in the main body of the work. They can include other emails/ memos, letters, reports, graphs, tables, charts, complex calculations, raw data and financial analyses.

If you do choose to include attachments/links in your work, make sure they are accurate and, for hyperlinks, functioning as of the day you send your document. A table, chart or graph with incorrect data can take away from your credibility, and a nonfunctioning hyperlink will annoy your reader AND create doubt about your work. Be wary of slow loading attachments or links — these can cause your reader/viewer to become impatient and give up, which may mean they do not return to your original text or return annoyed and less open to your conclusions.

All attachments should be clearly labeled, and any table, graph or chart you include should be accompanied by a legend, so the reader can fully understand the information you are trying to present. Most importantly, all attachments and links should clearly illustrate the point you are trying to make: attachments are designed to highlight the ideas in the main text, and they should never include extraneous or irrelevant data which will distract or confuse the reader. For example, if you have a table which illustrates additional variables other than the ones you are discussing, extract the necessary data and create a new table (unless, of course, the other variables provide needed context.)

5. Graphs and Tables

Graphs and tables are two ways to illustrate ideas in a written document. They can easily be produced using widely available software such as Excel. It is a good idea to experiment with different formats for presenting your data so that you can find the format that ***most clearly*** presents the information. One dimension of clarity is simply visual: It is important to keep in mind how the data will be viewed; for example, will readers see the table or graph on the printed page, or on a small screen, or will it be projected in an auditorium?

Another important dimension of clarity relates to your purpose in including the graph or table to begin with: does the graph or table present the information so that a reader/viewer can quickly identify the relevant factors and draw a conclusion from the data that matches your argument? If not, then maybe the graph or table format needs to be revised — assuming your data *does in fact* support your argument .

- You can include graphs or tables within the text of your document, as exhibits or appendices, or you can include them as attachments/links.
- You can also use graphs and tables as the centerpiece of your written document.

If the results of a project can best be illustrated by a graph or a table, then present that formatted data within the body of the document, surrounded by/hyperlinked to accompanying text. This method works best for a project which involves a lot of numerical data or when comparing and contrasting a number of options or recommendations.

Numerical data is best illustrated in table or graph form, so the reader can get a better sense of any trends the data depicts. The comparison of various options in table form allows you to list the pros and cons as well as the specific features of the recommendations you are presenting.

IV The Document Itself: Format Options

1. Email

In the 21st Century, the vast majority of written business communication is in the form of **electronic mail—which is abbreviated as "email."** Email may be composed in different formats but most often resembles a "note"—as opposed to a "letter"—and depending on the intended reader and the subject, may be considered either a formal or semi formal message. In Section V, below, communication tone is discussed; here we review format.

Most email systems require the sender to provide (type in) the name and email of the recipient in the "To" line, and include other readers in the "CC" or "BCC" lines. ["CC" stands for "Carbon Copy" and "BCC" stands for "Blind Carbon Copy" which are terms describing the means by which multiple copies of early documents were created — by placing a sheet of "carbon paper" in between the original and the under-copy.] A person who is "bcc'd" on an email sees the names in the To and CC lines, but their own name does not appear: those other readers do NOT see that bcc'd person's name. Email etiquette is always evolving, and every organization has its own standards, so be sure to ask about this as you start any new job.

For example, you will need to learn when to CC/BCC which people, and you will need to learn how your team, boss and/or organization prefers to handle long email strings (a series of emails.) It is considered appropriate to continue to use the same heading for an ongoing email string as long as the discussion within the emails relates to the heading.

Most people prefer to start a new email if new topics are introduced. When this happens, take special care to CC and BCC the right people on your new email—perhaps some of the earlier names can be left off, and others should be added since the topic has changed.

As a general guideline, remember to **read over your email several times before sending it,** keeping in mind not only the intended recipients but also the possibility that others may see it. **Do not put into email anything that is derogatory, false, or likely to cause trouble for you or your supervisor.**

1.1 Subject line

Think carefully about the subject line of your email so that it will be noticed amidst the clutter of everyone's inboxes. Try to use your subject line as effectively as possible—for example, if your email needs a reply by a date certain, be sure to flag that in the subject line. If your email is a reply/continuation of an already existing subject line, you don't need to change the heading (though it may be helpful to remove the "Fwd"s if more than one has collected as the email has been moved around the organization.)

Note that in the examples, below, "COB" stands for Close of Business—usually 5pm local time but your office may have different standards, especially if your business is a 24/7 global enterprise. Another common abbreviation is EOD (End of Day)—which may also mean something very specific depending on the norms of your employer.

Here are some examples of subject lines that advance your message:
- Subject: Meeting Weds 5/15 at 3pm: Confirmed
- Subject: Meeting Weds 5/15: TIME CHANGE
- Subject: Meeting next week: Must reschedule
- Subject: Pls review text updates for DJT Proposal: revisions due by Weds 5/15
- Subject: PLS REPLY: URGENT FOR TODAY COB
- Subject: Draft DJT proposal: edits, comments welcome before COB 5/15

1.2 Text of email:

For an email, as opposed to a letter (see next section), you do not need to include an address block at the upper left of the page. Instead, you start the email with the salutation that fits the person and the situation, as follows:

- **person is unknown to you and outside your organization:**
  - Dear Mr. Jones,

    I am writing to introduce myself and my firm to you on the recommendation of Sally Sanders, whom I met at the USTA conference last month.

- **person is unknown to you/inside your organization:**
  - Hi John Jones,

    I am Will Smith and I work with Debbie Daniels in purchasing. I am writing to follow up on your request that we identify a new vendor....

- **person is known to you but may be higher in rank or not a close friend:**
  - Hi Bill,

    I hope this email finds you well. I am writing to ask if we might find some time to meet this week or next week to review the standards for the new RFP relating to....

- **person is well known to you/is a friend:**
  - Hi Jane: We can't meet Weds as proposed but Thursday at 10 am works for me and my team, will that work for you guys? If not, lets look at next week—we are pretty open Monday all day and Tuesday before 2pm...
  - Hey Jane: Yes, Weds is good for lunch at 12—see you in the lobby!
  - Jane: Do you have 2 min to talk? Call me!

2. Letters

Letters are more formal documents, formatted with an address block on the upper left side of the page. Business letters usually include footer identification (words or numbers) to enable others to find them in the firm's computer system, and while the letter may be sent electronically, there will usually be a paper copy generated so that the sender can sign the letter before it is scanned for digital transmission.

Many companies will prepare formal letters to accompany proposals to potential clients; the format of a standard business letter is the most neutral and professional way to present information.

3. Memos

Memo formats may depend on whether you are writing them to print on paper or sending them electronically, and in fact your firm may have a pre-printed template for you to use that provides the headings. Generally, a memo has a heading that includes a subject line (RE: which stands for "Regarding") and then the text of the document begins below the subject line, often without any further salutation, as follows:

To: John Jones, Regional Vice President

From: Bill Smith, Director, Customer Service

Date: May 15, 2018

RE: Updates to Summer Delivery Schedules

As requested, I have had my team update the summer delivery schedules in the system so that everyone can see them when placing their product orders for clients. Hopefully, with this information easy to find, sales reps will not promise deliveries for weeks when we cannot deliver.

4. Reports

Reports are usually longer documents you have been directed to prepare (or you are helping your supervisor prepare,) that summarize information that decision-makers need. They may have several sections, including possibly an Executive Summary, and may include appendices or exhibits. See Section II (above) for detailed advice on the content for reports. The format for different sections of a report will reflect the content of that section. For example, there may be a cover letter as a formal introduction or as an Executive Summary, followed by sections that are numbered chronologically, with supporting documents using alphabetical tabs located after the numbered sections.

V Effective Communication: Tone Fits Purpose and Audience

As noted above in Section I regarding how to address emails to different people, it makes sense to match your tone to your purpose and to your audience. If you are writing something for your clients, coworkers and/or bosses, the tone should be earnest, serious and straightforward. You are trying to write as clearly and concisely as possible, and you are hoping to convey to the reader that you have a command of your subject.

Active or Passive Voice: When writing in English, you must choose the "active" or "passive" voice, and you will want to match the voice in each sentence of a business document to your objectives. As noted earlier in section II, when you are requesting something from someone it can be useful to use the active voice, however when drafting it is always advisable to consider not only your own objectives but also your relationship to the reader.

Criticism: If you are writing to offer criticism, be very careful and **if at all possible, offer your criticisms orally and not in writing.** If you have to write critically, be sensitive to the following issues:

■ You should frame your comments carefully, since the recipient may not believe that you are qualified to offer criticism. Limit your comments to the areas where you have real credibility and/or authority to offer feedback and advice to the person;

■ You should write as tactfully as possible and try to offer positive support along with any criticism;

■ You should consider showing your critical remarks to a third party (if possible without compromising confidentiality) to ensure that they are not going to give inadvertent offense; and

■ You must keep in mind that anything in writing could be shared, so be sure that you can defend your points and that your comments will not hurt you if they are read by supervisors or colleagues other than the intended recipient.

Just as you should never write anything derogatory, false or likely to cause trouble for your supervisor or teammates, similarly you should not send emails with jokes or links to supposedly funny things. You should avoid humor, such as jokes, funny comments or links to funny things on the Internet because, while you may find the item in question humorous, you really do not know what others will think—and there is too big a risk of offending someone inadvertently.

And, equally as important, you simply don't know who might see the email if it is forwarded onward. And another very important point about forwarding any email is to **_be sure to review the entire email before forwarding_** in case there is troublesome material at the bottom of the email.

Remember: You have control over what you write. Avoid creating problems for yourself—and do not contribute to email strings that others may send you where there is questionable content.

Do not put into writing anything that you would not want to see published on the front page of the newspaper that your boss reads each morning.

VI Social Media

In Chapter Two there are instructions for cleaning up your digital footprint; here I want you to think about how you use social media both personally and professionally. When you start a job, and depending on your role, there may be approved and/or disapproved social media practices and the burden is on you as the new employee to find out what you should and should not do, now that you work there.

Since there are fewer and fewer people who do not have a presence on Facebook or Linked In, Twitter, Instagram, Snapchat, etc., it is highly unlikely that you will be told not to use social media at all. What is more likely is that there will be a set of **guidelines that you will be asked to follow** regarding how you refer to your employer when you are online.

- You may be asked to restrict yourself when using your social media accounts to strictly personal comments, or you may be asked to refrain from posting anything (even anything personal) that could create an unfavorable impression of your employer.

- It may be helpful for you to add a disclaimer to your profiles, disassociating your comments from your employer, however, as noted in Chapter Two, **never assume that a disclaimer will shield you** if your employer is unhappy with anything you post online.

Many offices use chatroom apps like Campfire, HipChat, Yammer and Slacker—and there are real risks that you need to be aware of as you communicate on these platforms. Fundamentally, you need to always remember that **nothing is private** on any of these communication platforms (or new ones that may be released) unless it is encrypted/explicitly designed to be secure.

In other words, unless you are explicitly told otherwise, **assume that there is no privacy and no security on whatever software platforms that are being used for inter and intra office communication**—whether provided through a major company like Microsoft or Google, or through a proprietary app like Slacker.

It is critically important to always keep this lack of privacy and security foremost in your mind whenever you are communicating digitally because these applications are so easy to use that you can fall into complacency and write things that you—or your boss—would NOT want to see made public.

RF | Dean Lazar's Golden Tips

Golden Tip # 1
"You are what you repeatedly do. Excellence, then, is not an act but a habit."

—Aristotle

You decide your level of effort and your attention to detail. You will learn the most if you try your best to do A+ work, *even if it is not recognized or rewarded by others.* [page xvi]

Golden Tip # 2
Use the Resources Available to You.

If you are already out of school, go to the library or a local bookstore. Look around for mentors and advisors in your workplace and community. There is wisdom and experience all around you. [page 2]

Golden Tip #3
You Drive the CAR in Your Career.

Cultures and families are different, and some people feel obligated to pursue the profession chosen for them by their families. Whether or not you are paying your own college tuition, you are the person who will be living your life, and you must drive the career car. [page 5]

Golden Tip #4
Be Intentional and Strategic.

The world doesn't care if you succeed or not, so the burden is always on you

- To focus your attention,
- To continually motivate yourself, and
- To take steps that enable you to grow and prosper in your career.

[page 9]

Golden Tip #5
Think Globally, Act Locally.

The world needs you to care about social and economic justice, about natural resources and climate change, and about creating opportunities for everyone in our communities to live decent lives. [page 10]

Golden Tip #6
You Join an Ecosystem of Opportunity by Communicating With People.

Networking and socializing are the keys to finding your niche in the work ecosystem of your choice. [page 20]

Golden Tip #7
Build Your Own Personal Social Capital.

As you grow your professional network, your challenge will be to leverage these contacts. Don't underestimate the power of weak or loose ties. Build your own *personal social capital* by continuously investing time and attention in socializing and networking. [page 23]

Golden Tip #8
ABC = Always Be Connecting.

There is no substitute for face-to-face socializing when it comes to creating professional options, because your next opportunity can emerge directly or indirectly from someone you meet at an event. You invest in yourself every time you exchange contact information with someone new. [page 24]

Golden Tip #9
Practice Small Talk with Strangers.

Use any opportunities that present themselves to you to hone your small talk skills. Practice chatting people up on the line at the grocery store, on the bus, or in a waiting room. Smile, try to engage and be prepared to be rebuffed a few times—the times when you do get a positive response will more than make up for the times when people are not interested in talking with you. [page 25]

Golden Tip #10
Build Your Personal Board of Directors.

Find people willing to guide you in the future by being authentic and hard working in the present.
[page 30]

Golden Tip #11
Safeguard Your Reputation.

Think about the impacts of your words and actions BEFORE you speak or act. Here are two examples of the advice of sages, old and new:

- "Regard your good name as the richest jewel you possess—for credit is like fire; when once you have kindled it you may easily preserve is, but if you once extinguish it, you will find it an arduous task to rekindle it again. The way to gain a good reputation is to endeavor to be what you desire to appear."
  —Socrates (469 BC–399 BC)
- "It takes 20 years to build a reputation and five minutes to ruin it. If you think about that, you'll do things differently."
  —Warren Buffet

[page 31]

Golden Tip #12
Read, Read, Read.

Read widely in the professional journals in the fields you are interested in, keep up with relevant websites and blogs (does your professor write one?) and have some idea of what is happening in the world. Do not rely on television for your news. [page 33]

Golden Tip #13
Influence What Employers See About You Online.

Make a checklist of the adjectives you want employers to think of when they review you as a potential hire, use those words yourself when appropriate, and post things that will inspire others to use those words to describe you. [page 43]

Golden Tip #14
Copying Others is OK When It Comes to Keywords.

When you are completing an online profile you want to use a lot of keywords so that computer algorithms used by employers and recruiters will find you. Copy the keywords used by those who have the job(s) you want! [page 44]

Golden Tip #15
You Can't Turn Down What Hasn't Been Offered.

You have to get in the game, and pro-actively seek out opportunities that you are qualified for and interested in. Don't spend time worrying and deciding that you won't get picked and talk yourself out of applying. [page 47]

Golden Tip #16
Use your Minutes.

You may feel that your time is constrained by school, family and/or work commitments, and you may imagine that you are never free to "do what you want to do," but it is almost surely the case that you can control some portion of your time. *Be intentional and make good choices with those minutes, however few they may seem to be!* Over time, you can accomplish a lot working just a few minutes a day or week on a project or an idea. You can always learn something new — even something that seems insurmountably hard — if you break it into steps and apply yourself diligently over time. [page 49]

Golden Tip #17
Never Wear New Clothes (Especially New Shoes) to an Interview.

To be authentic and natural, you need to relax, and new clothes may be uncomfortable or cause you to move awkwardly. On the other hand, you certainly don't want to look scruffy or unkempt! Every season, region and workplace has a dress code — make sure that you only deviate from it in tasteful ways that do not inadvertently cause you to lose status. [page 63]

Golden Tip #18
To Fail to Prepare is to Prepare to Fail.

Don't sabotage yourself by neglecting to prepare for every interview. Focus on the things you can control: **learn** about your interviewer/the company/the industry, **plan** a conservative outfit and make sure it is clean and ready, **prepare** your best answers to likely questions relating to your academic studies, your work background and your interest in the position. [page 64]

Golden Tip #19
Express Appreciation Using your Words.

Thank you notes help you build your social vocabulary, and are an important part of building your personal social capital. Stay in touch with people who have met with you and helped you. Sending thank you letters is part of stepping up and taking responsibility for how people will remember you: were you sincere? Did you follow up? [page 66]

Golden Tip #20
It's Who You Know + What You Know.

We all know the cliché that getting ahead in life is all about who you know. While this Guide emphasizes networking to get ahead in your career, the truth is that building a great career is not only about who you know: *it's also about what you know.* All the networking in the world won't help you if you don't develop some real expertise and the capacity to make a contribution to the work of others. [page 70]

Golden Tip #21
Cultivate Your Curiosity.

Everyone always says you need to pursue your passion, but what if you aren't sure what your passion is? Don't worry about your passion and instead, cultivate your curiosity! Always be learning and engaging the world on your own terms, and you will make yourself into an interesting and successful person. [page 81]

Golden Tip #22
You Are Joining a Show Already in Progress.

There is a shared history/narrative in the workplace you are joining—be sure to learn your role in the ongoing production so you can demonstrate what a good fit you are for your job. Except for new start-ups, you will join an organization, a team, a hierarchy. Make sure you understand who is officially in charge, who has the real influence and what part you are playing in the show. [page 95]

Golden Tip #23
Think of It As "Me, Incorporated."

Successful careers are deliberate creations. You must take a business-like approach to your career, anticipate the obvious challenges, make decisions rationally, and take pro-active steps to ensure your success, happiness and financial well-being. Think of it as building a company that is called "Me, Inc." If not you, then who? [page 101]

Golden Tip #24
Life is Random, Your Response is Not.

Life may be a series of random occurrences of incalculable odds, but how you marshal your intelligence and your energy to respond to life's challenges is totally up to you. [page 110]

Golden Tip #25
You Are on Their Team but They Are NOT on Your Team.

Remember: It's Me Inc., no matter what your paycheck says. While the employer paying you rightfully expects your professional loyalty, this does not mean that you should trust them with any of your *personal* dreams, plans or ideas. Never share your thoughts about a potential job change, a move out of town or overseas, or plans for going back to school—until you are literally ready to resign. [page 120]

Golden Tip #26
You Are Not A Robot.

Only robots work 24/7. Take vacations, spend time with friends. No one can or should be always on, always networking, always seeking their next opportunity. There are going to be days, weeks and months when you should just do your job and create good work that impresses your supervisors and showcases your abilities. [page 134]

Golden Tip #27
You Get What You Give.

Is the glass half full or half empty? Are you an optimist or a pessimist? However you feel about the world, remember that when you are interacting with people, they see and react to what you show them. If you offer a positive outlook on life, a can-do attitude, and a smile, you will generally get a better response than if you scowl and present yourself as critical, disappointed or disillusioned. [page 141]

Golden Tip #28
Remember ABC: Be Authentic, Be a Builder, Be a Collaborator.

Being authentic in the context of work means talking the talk and walking the walk of a *builder and collaborator* who respects the contributions of others. One mark of a team player is that they never take all the credit for the work of their group — they talk about *our efforts* and *our success*. [page 142]

Golden Tip #29
Be Punctual, Prepared and Present.

Employers actually do notice the staff who are eager to do well, and often offer special opportunities to team members who are in the office early. Being present means listening actively when you are talking with someone: *listen with your eyes* and *smile to show you are getting the point.* [page 144]

Golden Tip #30
Don't Let Fear Sabotage You.

Everyone has insecurities about presenting themselves as an expert — everyone suffers at one time or another from so-called *imposter syndrome.* It is important to face the future without fear so you can find the inner strength to face challenges and seize opportunities when they present themselves. Over time, you will become more confident as you live and work in the world. As the Nike slogan, says, *Just Do It.* [page 145]

Golden Tip #31
Dysfunctional Organizations Defeat People.

It is a universally recognized rule of business life that *when a highly functional person meets a dysfunctional organization, the organization wins.* Don't take it personally — as soon as you realize the problem, decide to learn whatever you can in the situation and get yourself a new job as quickly as you can! [page 147]

Index

Alcohol, 37, 113, 114, 121

alumni, 25, 32, 44, 48, 72, 82, 86–88, 98, 144, 188, 194

appearance, 11, 63

Aristotle, xvi, 110, 135

Arts Administration, 5

Ashoka, 100

authentic, 30, 63, 65, 141, 142, 144, 175

Best practices, xv, 47, 117, 170, 181

Bureau of Labor Statistics, 2, 159

business cards, 27, 29

Caffeine, 114,

careerism, 143

circumstances of birth, 145

code switching, 104

commercial business, 5, 20

company culture, 85, 92

corporate America, 86

consulting, 5, 115, 162

cooking, 116, 117

counseling, 5, 176

cover letters, 50, 52, 57, 59, 78

critical thinking, 125, 126, 156

data, 2, 42, 73, 85, 149, 160, 168

data analytics, 60, 73, 76–78, 168

databases, 44, 53, 58, 88, 163

digital footprint, 38, 40, 120, 139, 155, 213

downsizing, 86

drugs, 114

downtime, 112, 116

education, xvi, 5, 73, 74, 99, 123, 146, 147, 152, 159, 163, 182, 186

elevator speech, 14, 15, 18, 141

entrepreneurial centers, 98

exercise, 112, 113, 116

Facebook, 36, 38–40, 42, 45, 78, 104, 117, 119, 120, 213

feedback, 23, 30, 128, 131–133, 169, 212

fear, 1, 22, 145, 173

Google, 37, 41, 42, 88, 130

habits, xv, 70, 81, 101, 111, 112, 117, 128, 133, 135, 145, 152, 153, 175, 189

helping others, 141

imposter syndrome, 145

Indeed.com, 8, 160

informational interview, 23, 84, 88, 91, 123, 143, 191

information overload, 77

Instagram, 36, 37, 45, 213

intellectual challenge, 9

intentional, 1, 6, 7, 9, 10, 33, 39, 44, 49, 54, 151, 177

interview, xvi, 8, 11, 12, 23, 33, 48–50, 53, 57, 63–67, 69, 78, 84, 86, 88, 90–94, 123, 141–143, 174, 176, 191, 194

internet sites, 2, 8, 159

interpersonal skills, 4, 6, 134

introductory narratives, 14

journalism, 5

key words, 90, 167

kindred spirits, 130

low residency degree programs, 75

management, 5, 6, 39, 67, 83, 85–87, 96, 97, 99, 102, 122, 123, 128, 135, 161, 183

marketing, 5, 18, 19, 32, 85

market research, 5, 18

marijuana, 114, 115

Medium, 77, 91

mental health counselors, 103, 107, 112

mindfulness, 116, 135

mistakes, 56, 64, 109, 131, 132, 138, 144, 145, 171, 192

mock interviews, 8

MOOCs, 74

Musk, Elon, 124, 156

narratives, 4, 14, 15, 19, 23, 51, 144

non-cognitive skills, 128

nonprofit, 5, 20, 32, 93, 99, 100, 150, 151, 153, 160

non-traditional credentials, 73

on campus recruiting, 82

online presence, 12, 36, 38–41, 44, 45, 54, 139

operations analysis, 5, 77, 83, 85, 86, 185

opportunity benefit, 72

opportunity cost, 71, 72, 98, 181, 188

opportunity ecosystem, 20

Passion, 1, 65, 66, 81, 113, 137

performance review, 86, 132, 133

personal brand, 39

personas, 35, 37

Pinterest, 36, 45

positive thinking, 15, 109

privacy settings, 38

product development, 5, 92, 185

public speaking, 13, 63, 171, 173

recruitment, 5, 82, 193

Reddit, 36, 119

relationships, xiv, 2, 22, 30, 72, 98, 128, 134, 140, 143, 170, 171, 199

reputational dangers, 36, 45

resilience, 22, 70, 107, 112, 113, 128, 134

resumes, 45, 56, 57, 59, 73, 89

robots, 76, 134, 138

salaries, 86, 99, 150

sales, 5, 83, 85, 92

search process, 48

search terms, 54

self care, 40, 113, 136

self nurturing, 113

self presentation, 12, 19, 23

self respect, 110, 128, 129, 131, 146

self talk, 109, 129, 144
selling yourself, 49
social entrepreneurs, 100, 150
social justice, 11

technology, best practices, 117
Twitter, 6, 36, 37, 39, 45, 77, 78, 213

Weibo, 36

YouTube, 36, 45

Made in the USA
Lexington, KY
13 September 2018